1
Fruits of
Medjugorje

The
Fruits of
Medjugorje

Stories of True
and Lasting Conversion

Elizabeth Ficocelli

Paulist Press
New York/Mahwah, N.J.

Excerpts from the monthly messages from Medjugorje come from the official Medjugorje website, www.medjugorje.hr, run by the Information Centre "Mir" Medjugorje, and from *Messages from Heaven* (St. James Publishing). Both are used with permission.

Cover photos by Joe Mixan. Used with permission.

Cover design by Sharyn Banks
Book design by Lynn Else

Library of Congress Cataloging-in-Publication Data

Ficocelli, Elizabeth.
    The fruits of Medjugorje : stories of true and lasting conversion / Elizabeth Ficocelli.
        p. cm.
    Includes bibliographical references.
    ISBN 0-8091-4388-7 (alk. paper)
    1. Mary, Blessed Virgin, Saint—Apparitions and miracles—Bosnia and Hercegovina—Medjugorje. 2. Medjugorje (Bosnia and Hercegovina)—Religious life and customs. 3. Religious awakening—Catholic Church. 4. Catholic converts. I. Title.
    BT660.M44F53 2006
    232.91'70949742—dc22

                                                            2005028978

Published by Paulist Press
997 Macarthur Boulevard
Mahwah, New Jersey 07430

www.paulistpress.com

Printed and bound in the
United States of America

Contents

*This book is dedicated
to the Queen of Peace,
mother of us all.*
E.F.

"Are grapes gathered from thorns, or figs from thistles? In the same way, every good tree bears good fruit, but the bad tree bears bad fruit. A good tree cannot bear bad fruit, nor can a bad tree bear good fruit. Every tree that does not bear good fruit is cut down and thrown into the fire. Thus you will know them by their fruit." Matthew 7:16–20

"Dear children, behold...I want to call you to start living a new life as of today. Dear children, I want you to comprehend that God has chosen each one of you, in order to use you in a great plan for the salvation of mankind. You are not able to comprehend how great your role is in God's design. Therefore, dear children, pray so that in prayer you may be able to comprehend what is God's plan in your regard. I am with you in order that you may be able to bring it about in all its fullness. Thank you for having responded to my call."

First monthly message to the world
from Our Lady of Medjugorje, January 25, 1987

Acknowledgments

This book is the result of a combination of efforts under what I believe to be the inspired guidance of Our Lady of Medjugorje. I am eternally grateful for the willingness of so many people to candidly share their personal conversion stories in the pages of this book, so that others may appreciate the abundance of good fruits attributed to the most important apparitions of our time. I would be remiss, however, if I didn't express my gratitude to a few special individuals in particular.

The first is June Klins, editor of *The Spirit of Medjugorje Newsletter*. I had the good and providential fortune of being put in contact with June early in my search for stories and found her to be an absolute gold mine of information. June willingly opened her heart and her newsletter archives, sharing stories and leads from which I could springboard. She did not do this for any personal credit or gain, but simply to fulfill the mission of spreading the messages of Medjugorje. I would also like to recognize the helpful input of Mary Sue Eck, editor of *Medjugorje Magazine*, Ana Shawl, cyber editor of *The Medjugorje Web*, and Carolanne Kilichowski for her source of leads as well. To complement the beautiful stories, Our Lady led me to Joe Mixan, firefighter and photographer, whose photographs grace the cover of this book. To me, his pictures speak more than a thousand words.

Duly noted is the love and understanding of my husband, Mark, and my four sons, Michael, Nicholas, Daniel, and Matthew, who patiently put up with seeing the back of my head for several months as I tapped away incessantly on my computer.

And last, but certainly not least, I wish to acknowledge the help and inspiration of my Divine Parents. God, the good and loving Father, overlooked my unworthiness and gave me this assignment because He knew I would accept the challenge. In typical father fashion, He expects much from His children. In my weaker moments of panic, wondering how I could do justice to such an important work, in what seemed an impossibly short time, I would feel the gentle reassurance of the Blessed Mother. She lovingly and consistently brought me story after story, helping me to overcome obstacles and make the interviewing, writing, and editing process a true joy. Like a good mother, she was careful not to overwhelm her fragile daughter by burdening her with too many stories at once or revealing to her the full scope of the project in the beginning. Instead, it was given to me piece by piece, with clear affirmations along the way to let me know that this was *her* project and that everything was under control. I can honestly say with all humility that the experience of writing this book has taken my faith relationship with the Virgin Mary to a much deeper level. As a former Protestant with a previously reverent but at-arm's-length relationship with the Immaculate Conception, I now see her as a loving and understanding mother. For that discovery alone, this book has been worth all the effort.

Introduction

Twenty-five years ago, an astounding claim was made that the Mother of God was appearing daily to six Croatian youngsters in the remote hamlet of Medjugorje (Med-joo-gor-ee-ah), in the geographic region now well-known to the world as Bosnia-Herzegovina. The news was worthy enough to grace the covers of prestigious publications such as *Life, Newsweek,* the *Boston Globe,* and *Reader's Digest,* and even earn segments on television shows such as *20/20, Unsolved Mysteries, Inside Edition, Geraldo,* and *Sally Jesse Raphael.*

It is estimated that since the events were first reported in 1981, more than 20 million people from around the world have traveled to this obscure village—even in the midst of a bloody civil war—to experience firsthand a unique meeting of heaven and earth. The Madonna's message that God exists and the repeated call for conversion through her consistent pleas for prayer, fasting, peace, and reconciliation seem to find receptive ears beyond the expected Catholic audience. Protestants, Jews, and even Muslims can be counted among the masses that flood this rural community year after year. Some come with broken bodies. Others come with broken spirits. Still others come out of curiosity, hoping to witness supernatural phenomena. Almost everyone who comes to Medjugorje, however, leaves the same way: spiritually strengthened and meaningfully converted.

The intention of this book is to focus on the fruits of Medjugorje only, not to address the claims of other contemporary visions. However, it is important to note that the proliferation of supernatural reports today from various parts of the globe has seemed to foster an attitude of indifference or even skepticism among many when it comes to the subject of apparitions.

Today, the very name *Medjugorje* elicits a wide range of emotions, from passionate devotion to cool caution to heated opposition. Because so many years have elapsed since the visions were first reported, it seems that everyone can form, and has formed, a firm opinion of what is actually taking place there, but the opinion that holds weight in the end—at least for Catholics—is that of the Catholic Church. Normal protocol regarding events like these is for the Church to turn the investigation process over to the local hierarchy. In the case of Medjugorje, there have been complexities in this process. The local bishop has retracted his initial favorable opinion about the apparitions, some claim because of political dispute between the diocese and the local Franciscans, or because of the pressure of the Communist government. During a conference of Yugoslavian bishops, a special commission was appointed to continue investigations and settle the controversy once and for all. After years of study, the commission concluded that it could not affirm the supernatural nature of these apparitions. However, neither could it prove them false. Whether they liked this answer or not, the bishops in the region have agreed on one thing: to assume responsibility for the pastoral care of the staggering numbers of faithful that visit Medjugorje year after year. Their primary concern today is that liturgical practices and

Marian devotion are promoted in accordance with the teachings of the Church.

A further complication in the matter of Medjugorje is that the apparitions are ongoing, a radical departure from traditional visions such as Fatima, Lourdes, Knock, and La Sallette, which lasted a few short days or weeks. Twenty-five years later, three of the six Medjugorje visionaries still have daily apparitions; the other three receive one apparition a year and were told by Our Lady they would do so for the rest of their lives.

Because of the ongoing phenomenon, it would be imprudent for the Church to authenticate the events at this time. Yet she cannot turn her back to the fact that interest in Medjugorje is anything but diminishing. In fact, it has become the fastest-growing Marian place of pilgrimage in the world today. In an article by Antonio Gaspari in the November 1996 issue of *Inside the Vatican,* it is claimed that more confessions are heard at St. James Church in Medjugorje than in any other parish in the world, keeping more than 150 confessors busy every day. In 1990, at the peak of political unrest and just prior to the outbreak of civil war, 1,900,000 people received Communion in Medjugorje, surpassing even the popular shrine of Fatima. It is reported that more than 30,000 priests and bishops have visited the Croatian village and that the apparitions have spawned hundreds of active prayer groups around the world. Even the late pontiff John Paul II expressed positive sentiments about Medjugorje and a personal desire to go there. A papal visit is not possible, however, until the apparitions have ended and the Church has granted her authority.

When the visionaries, at the request of the local priests, questioned the Virgin in 1986 about the matter of being obedient to the Church and obedient to the call of God, her answer was straightforward:

> *"One must follow the authority of the Church with certainty. Yet, before she expresses an opinion, it is necessary to advance spiritually, because she will not be able to express a judgement in a vacuum, but in a confirmation which presupposes growth of the child. First comes birth, followed by Baptism, then Confirmation. The Church comes to confirm him, who is born of God. We must walk and advance in the spiritual life, affected by these messages."*

This revealing statement is the inspiration for this book. As is the case with all apparitions, the Church must examine the overall fruits of Medjugorje in order to arrive at an accurate conclusion. Exhaustive scientific and psychological tests have already been performed on the visionaries, who are now married adults with children living in Bosnia, Italy, and America. Documented medical miracles also have been associated with Medjugorje. It is now time to look at the true and lasting spiritual changes that are occurring in people's hearts because of the Virgin's invitation to prayer and fasting, Eucharist, Confession, Holy Scripture, and peace. How are these hearts, set afire, inspiring people to live the Gospel of Jesus Christ in a world seemingly devoid of peace? This is the real test of any series of apparitions; these are the stories the world needs to hear.

This book is an attempt to present a small sampling of the millions of people who have been profoundly converted by Medjugorje, and who are living witnesses to their conversion today. For many, the impact of the messages has spawned surprising new ministries and direction. For some, it has led to the discovery—or rediscovery—of religious vocations. Still others have been called to spread the messages through a variety of artistic endeavors, including print and broadcast media, music, theater, and video production. The book has been written in a spirit to bring healing, understanding, and balance to a controversial subject that continues to breed confusion among Catholic clergy and laity today. For the lukewarm or the skeptical, my intention is to present credible evidence that the apparitions of Medjugorje are bringing peace, holiness, and renewed faith to the world since 1981. For those who already accept and believe, I pray that the book will encourage an honest self-evaluation to determine if we are truly applying the messages in our own lives, or if we are in need of a renewed sense of mission. Finally, my hope is that this book can present the Church with substantial confirmation of the good fruit that is produced when the messages of Medjugorje are applied diligently and lived out with sincerity, charity, and humility.

As those who have been privileged to visit Medjugorje will attest, it is an oasis of glorious worship and profound peace. Some have described their pilgrimage to this special place as an encounter with heaven itself. It is not surprising, therefore, that most people who travel to Medjugorje feel a certain reluctance to return home. It is also not uncommon for people to make multiple pilgrimages to this holy corner of the world or even live there for a time. But coming home to "reality," as difficult as it might be, and discovering oneself changed in an otherwise unchanged world is exactly what these apparitions are challenging us to do. In Holy Scripture, Jesus retreated to the mountains to seek time alone with God for spiritual support and direction. We, like Jesus, also may find ourselves called to ascend the mountains of Podbrdo and Krizevac in Medjugorje for a personal encounter with the Divine. But, also like Our Lord and Savior, we must come down from these mountains with joyful and awakened hearts, prepared to go out to a hurting world and share the Good News. There is an obligation to those who have heard the messages of the Virgin. If we selfishly harbor the blessings of Medjugorje for our own personal growth only, we have missed the point entirely.

I have been compelled to take on this rather controversial project for two reasons. The first is that I, like countless others, have received the messages of Medjugorje and the invitation of Our Lady to live these words and share them with the world. As scripture tells us, to those who have been given much, much will be expected. Second, as a Catholic convert and author, I have discovered through prayerful discernment that I am called to use my writing to help educate and enthuse Catholics about their faith and lead them into deeper relationship with God. I credit my own pilgrimage to Medjugorje in 1989, six years after my entrance into the Church, for accelerating exponentially my budding faith. During the years prior to my pilgrimage, I had immersed myself in studying Catholicism, including Church history, lives of the saints, doctrine, and mystical events. I was already accepting and appreciative of God's grand display of exterior signs of faith seemingly reserved for the Catholic faithful, such as stigmata, visions, and eucharistic miracles. Therefore, the concept of a supernatural phenomenon occurring in my lifetime was not an obstacle to my faith, but an opportunity to expand it.

Medjugorje has moved me from studying and admiring my faith to *living* it. It has inspired me to attend Mass during the week in addition to Sundays and has prompted me to move from occasional Confession to monthly Reconciliation. Medjugorje has fed me with the spiritual strength to incorporate weekly fasts of bread and water. And, not insignificantly, it has fostered in this former Protestant a substantial relationship with the Mother of God.

In comparison to other people's pilgrimages to Medjugorje, mine was rather typical. I experienced the spinning of the sun, rosaries turning gold, and a physical healing for a member of our family. For me, these experiences were simply exterior confirmations that something special was happening in this part of the world. Medjugorje was also my first exposure to the Universal Church coming together to worship with one voice expressed in many languages, praising God with exuberant song and prayer that practically lifted the roof off St. James Church. This, I remember thinking to myself, is what worship is *supposed* to be. In my imagination, it was the closest imitation on earth to the celestial celebration awaiting us in heaven.

God spoke to my heart often during my eight days in Medjugorje, but nowhere louder than in the confessional, which continues to be the case for me today. I went to make the sacrament of Reconciliation early in my pilgrimage, not because I felt I had a lot to confess, but because I had read that many people experience their first true confession in Medjugorje. As a convert, I was still wrestling with this sacrament, so I apprehensively searched for the confessional marked "English."

The line was relatively short and I felt encouraged as I waited in place, trying to stay warm that cold December afternoon. Stone churches, I discovered, had an uncanny knack for keeping in the cold. As I waited, I read some passages from a small blue book, *Pray with the Heart,* by Father Slavko Barbaric, and tried to prepare myself for making a heartfelt confession. In between meditations, I kept checking my watch. An hour and a half had gone by, and I did not seem to be much closer to the confessional. The man behind me in line told me that the priest we were waiting to speak to was Father Philip Pavich, an American priest who had spent twelve years in Jerusalem before requesting a transfer to Medjugorje. The man also told me that his first confession with Father Philip had taken more than an hour. I was dumbfounded. I couldn't possibly imagine what someone could talk about for that length of time.

As I inched forward in line, the five o'clock Rosary began, which marked the beginning of the evening activity at St. James. Every night, the Rosary is prayed from 5:00 to 6:00 p.m. and the apparitions occur at about 5:40 p.m. In the days when the children had their visions in the choir loft of the church, the priest leading the Rosary would abruptly stop praying for a few minutes, a signal that the apparitions were occurring at that time. Since the children were now having their apparitions in their homes or elsewhere, there was no obvious indication in the church when the visions were actually taking place.

By now I was growing quite frustrated that Father Philip was taking so long with the people ahead of me. In my complete naiveté, I was concerned about being in the confessional during the time of the apparition. I wanted to be out in the church with the others in case something "happened." But that was not to be; by the time it was my turn to confess, the apparition was only minutes away. I was at first somewhat distracted by the appearance of the confessor sitting across from me. He looked more like a rabbi than a priest, with his long black woolen robe and hat and his overgrown salt-and-pepper beard. I began the process by admitting I had nothing major to confess, only that perhaps I should be praying more and with better focus. He asked me about my marital status, how long I had been married, and if we had children. I told him that I had been married for almost five years and that we had elected to wait a while before starting a family. Seeing disapproval on Father Philip's face, I quickly pointed out that my husband and I were using Natural Family Planning (NFP), and figured that this would earn points with him. Instead, Father Philip began to upbraid me in no uncertain terms. He told me that using NFP to postpone conception for such a long time was deliberately closing God out on an important part of our lives, and by doing this we were adopting a pagan attitude. This caught me completely off guard. I felt confused and overwhelmed, and I wanted out. The more he talked, the more I cried.

As tears fell from my downcast eyes onto my tightly clenched, mittened hands, I happened to catch sight of my watch and was suddenly reminded of the upcoming apparition. The time was exactly 5:40 p.m. At that moment, I had a sensation inside me of a light being switched on, followed by a rush of warmth in the otherwise cold confessional. I heard a faint buzzing sound and thought that perhaps someone had opened up the confessional next to us, but when I stumbled out of the little wooden booth, dazed and lightheaded, I saw that there was no confessional on the other side of us—ours was the last one in the row.

The 6:00 p.m. Croatian Mass was about to get underway, and I spotted my family sitting in the pews. By now I had transitioned from feeling shocked and overwhelmed to feeling downright angry. I tried to push my feelings aside and focus on the Mass, but it was impossible. My husband noticed that I was visibly distraught and he took me out to the courtyard. I told him about my Confession and how Father Philip had challenged us. We were both upset by the man's forthrightness, and completely opposed to his strong advice for us to stop postponing conception. This was not what we had come halfway around the world to hear. As the week of our pilgrimage unfolded, however, my husband and I received several indications that, indeed, this message was meant for us to receive, reflect on, and obey. By the end of the week, our hardened hearts had softened. We were ready to turn back to God and give Him the authority and control He desired in our lives.

The Virgin Mary's underlying theme in Medjugorje is about surrendering ourselves to God and living His plan, not ours. Yet I was oblivious to the meaning of that in my own life until I made my pilgrimage. Through Medjugorje, the Blessed Mother taught me that surrender and conversion are for everyone. And so my husband and I returned home with a new mindset. We continued charting our monthly fertility cycle, but we gingerly gave up control to God. A few months later, a home pregnancy test told me that I was carrying a new life. When we checked our charts to see when we had conceived, we were amazed and delighted to discover that it was on June 25, the anniversary of the apparitions of Medjugorje.*

---

* The Virgin Mary first appeared in Medjugorje on June 24, 1981, the feast of John the Baptist, a fitting occasion since she had come to tell the world that God exists. She did not speak to the children until the second day, June 25, which is considered the unofficial feast day of the apparitions. Stories in this book will refer to both dates.

My story is small compared to the ones you are about to read. But for me, a new child (followed by three more, the third of whom was actually born on June 25) was the first of many important ways in which my life would be forever changed because of Medjugorje. That one pilgrimage, so many years ago, will always remain emblazoned in my heart and in my mind. I am a Catholic alive in my faith, in love with the Lord and the Blessed Mother, and longing to tell the world about it. I truly believe this planet has been anointed in holiness for the past twenty-five years with messages from heaven, and that we are better people because of it. Savor the following stories of how so many have experienced this anointing and have been made new. Immerse yourself in God's abundant love and mercy, and may it inspire a true and lasting conversion in your own heart.

Elizabeth Ficocelli
April 4, 2005
Solemnity of the Annunciation of the Lord

Prayer and Fasting

*"Dear children! Today I call
you to renew prayer and fasting with
even greater enthusiasm until prayer becomes a
joy for you. Little children, the one who prays is not
afraid of the future and the one who fasts is not afraid
of evil. Once again, I repeat to you: only through prayer
and fasting also wars can be stopped—wars of your unbe-
lief and fear for the future. I am with you and am teaching you, little children: your peace and hope are in God.
That is why draw closer to God and put Him in the
first place in your life. Thank you for having
responded to my call."*
Message of January 25, 2001

1

True Freedom

I spent eighteen years of my life in prison serving time for serious crimes such as murder, attempted murder, armed robbery, assault and battery, and escape. My life was on a path of self-destruction, satiated in every vice imaginable, and I cared for no one, most especially myself. Toward the end of those eighteen years, however, I was set free from my life of imprisonment—not by mere earthly parole, but by heavenly intercession.

It was spring of 1988 and I was two months shy of parole for an attempted murder charge at West Tennessee State Penitentiary. During a routine headcount one afternoon, my cell partner and I were watching a PBS program that showed six children on their knees, intently staring upward. They were mouthing words without sound and when their voices returned it was in a foreign language that I didn't understand. The narrator was saying something about the Blessed Virgin Mary. I had no idea what the program was about because I had been away from the Catholic Church for many years. I watched for a while and asked my cell partner what he thought about it. He didn't even know who the Blessed Virgin Mary was.

A few mornings later, I was walking the yard with a friend. He was in his head and I was in mine and we were walking together silently. All of a sudden, a sort of pressure, as best as I can describe it, came upon me. I thought I was going crazy, or at the very least having an acute anxiety attack. I wanted to run away, but I couldn't. I tried to talk to my friend to take my mind off it, but I couldn't speak. All I could do was continue to move in a forward direction, completely powerless under this mysterious pressure. I don't know how long this experience lasted; it seemed like forever, but it could have been an instant. I don't know. All I know is that in that moment, I understood that God existed. At the same time, I understood that there was a heaven and a hell. I didn't see any sort of vision; I just understood these things. Heaven was full of peace and happiness, but hell was a place of eternal suffering. It was ugly and there was no parole; you were there for the duration.

I saw myself in the light of God's justice and it was clear that I was standing on the brink of hell. For the first time in my life, this thought really scared me. I also understood I had to choose between the road that led to heaven or the one that led to hell. Quickly, I chose heaven, but I seemed to be repelled from this choice by an unseen force. This freaked me out even more. Again I was given the choice, and again I chose heaven, but as before, I was repelled. Then I understood that I wasn't really choosing heaven. I was trying to bend the road leading to hell and it wasn't working. With complete clarity, I saw that if I continued to live my life as I was doing, I would have to embrace the consequence: hell. The only other choice was to relinquish this road I was on and embrace that which would bring me to heaven. One by one, all my gods and vices appeared before my eyes and I had to let each and every one of them go. This is not to say I was totally free from them—far from it—but at that moment, being scared to death, I let them all go. It was like emptying a big trash bin full of garbage. At this point, the pressure eased off and I regained control of my body. I immediately walked back to my cell, ignoring my friend's questions, and just sat there, dumbstruck. Nothing like that had ever happened to me before. I don't think I could recreate that experience with any kind of drug.

Now, it wasn't like I got real religious all of a sudden, but for a few days I did experience a great sense of peace. I started to think a little about God, and when I did, I said a few prayers I remembered from my childhood. Then I learned that a priest was coming to the prison to say Mass, which was unusual because we were located in the Bible Belt. When he arrived, I asked him to hear my confession and I also received Holy Communion for the first time in many years. Each Thursday, the priest returned to say Mass and I was there. There was a greasy old rosary hanging on my cell wall that someone had given me long ago, and I began saying in private what I could remember of this prayer. I also felt compelled to give away all the drugs I had been dealing in prison.

On June 29, I was transported to Southern State Correctional Facility in New Jersey, a large prison complex consisting of five prison units on an expansive campus. Eighteen years earlier, I had been charged with murder in this state and narrowly escaped the electric chair. I was being sent back due to a parole violation on a thirty-year sentence for manslaughter. Upon arriving, I was pleased to discover that this prison had a Catholic chaplain and a regular Mass. One Saturday, an announcement was made that the Catholic Queen of Peace service was about to meet in the multi-purpose room. I was curious, so I went. It's important to realize how spiritually immature I was at this point. I had no clue about God's love or mercy. I saw God as a big cop up there ready to get me when I got out of line. I had been happily going off to hell until He came and threw a monkey wrench in the works, nearly frightening me to death. I was serving Him in complete fear to the point of anxiety attacks. I would go to Confession, walk away, and have to go back a few minutes later because I was sure He was going to zap me with a lightening bolt if I sinned. I was praying the Rosary and doing other religious practices just to get on His good side. The Catholic Queen of Peace service sounded like something that could earn me extra bonus points.

A group of little old ladies greeted us with rosary beads, religious materials, and a tray of cookies. Looking around, I figured most of the guys had shown up for the cookies. I had an attitude about people who claimed to discover religion in prison. They were often first-timers or sex offenders and they kept their heads buried in a Bible as a way to survive. It couldn't have been that important to them, because it was the one belonging they left behind after their release. To me they were phonies, and for that reason, I was quiet about what had happened to me back in Tennessee.

I prayed the Rosary with the group and, as I was leaving, one of the ladies handed me a newspaper entitled *The Miracle of Medjugorje* by Wayne Weible. I took it back to my area and read it, but I didn't believe what it said about the apparitions. I never believed in any of that stuff, nor did I have a devotion to the Blessed Mother. But there were a few suggestions in the paper that I started incorporating in my life to keep God off my back. These practices included praying seven Our Fathers, Hail Marys, and Glory Bes, seven Eternal Rests for the souls in purgatory, and regular fasting on bread and water. Something else that caught my attention in the newspaper was a quote from the Blessed Virgin Mary that said, *"Pray with your heart"* and *"Love the love that's in your heart."* I didn't know how to love anybody, not even myself, so when I walked around the prison, secretly praying the Rosary, I would ask the Blessed Mother what it meant to pray with your heart.

One of the favorite pastimes in prison was hanging out and sharing war stories about drugs, crimes, and women. Guys were always trying to top one another with their lurid tales, and I would often get sucked into the conversations because of peer pressure. One day I walked away from the group and started praying as I always did when I was alone. But this time I became aware that when I was praying, I was in God's presence. I also realized that I was in God's presence when I was talking with the guys. Feeling ashamed, I started avoiding the group and became ostracized because there was no place in prison to talk about holy things.

One evening I was out on the grounds, looking at my fellow inmates walking around empty and with no purpose. God was not in their lives, and to me, they were like walking dead people. I started praying for each and every one of them, asking God why He didn't zap them and make them know He was there. I was in tears begging for these guys. This is how Our Lady was teaching me to pray with my heart. I prayed more and tried to sacrifice more, taking on extra days of fasting. I began to pray with real intention and discovered that once I prayed with my heart, I could give up things with love. Eventually I got up the courage to ask God to let me serve Him out of love instead of fear.

I think God responded to me by opening my heart to Medjugorje. I had received another copy of the Wayne Weible newspaper from Father Hewett, the prison chaplain, who had become my friend and spiritual advisor. I took it back to my dorm and read it a second time, which was unheard of for me, and this time, it grabbed me. I believed. When I asked Father what he thought about it, he said he had been to Medjugorje and witnessed profound conversions and peace there, but he would submit to the final judgment of the Church. He also mentioned that he was going back again the following week.

While I knew it was impossible for me to go to Medjugorje, I started to think about sending something over there to be blessed. I figured Our Lady was a mom, she wouldn't zap anybody. She *invited* the children and never forced them. The children described how beautiful Our Lady was, especially her eyes. I wanted those eyes to pierce through the garbage in my soul so I could open up and love God and remove forever the fear in my heart.

I remembered I had a scapular of Our Lady of Mount Carmel in my pocket. My mother had sent it to me back in 1981 when I was living a very sinful life in Florida. When I had opened up the envelope, I didn't know what it was, but I put it on because the back of it said that whoever wore it would not suffer eternal fire. The string on the scapular had broken that same night, so I carried it in my pocket from then on; I wanted to keep it with me because it was from my mother. Father Hewett took my scapular to Medjugorje and had the visionary Vicka pray over it. While he was gone, I got the prayers for a scapular investment from the Queen of Peace ladies and I prepared myself properly. Upon Father Hewett's return, I repaired the broken string and had him formally invest me with the blessed scapular.

Within a week, a powerful love for Our Lady blossomed in me and it seemed I could not do enough for her. I decided to be patient and even courteous with people in prison who previously had infuriated me, offering it for Our Lady and her intentions. When I read about the little kids in Fatima and their voluntary mortifications out of love for the Virgin, I created my own "hair shirt" by taking wood splinters from the workshop where I worked and putting them in my sleeves. Unfortunately, I couldn't do any work this way, and Father Hewett released me from this practice.

I wanted to share my love for Our Lady and the news that God existed with all the guys in prison, but I still considered myself a respectable convict. I wasn't comfortable thumping the Bible. On occasion I would drag a few guys to Mass or to the Queen of Peace Rosary group, but they never stayed. As time went on, I desired to learn how to love Jesus the way He deserved to be loved, and to accept that He loved me even when I messed up (which I did quite frequently.) The ladies gave me some novenas, one of which was to St. Joseph. It sparked my interest because my middle name is Joseph and I am a carpenter by trade. I figured as the stepfather to the Lord, St. Joseph would have some clout. So I began the nine-day prayer, imploring this great saint to teach me to love Jesus as He deserved to be loved and to help me understand His love for me. The ninth day of the novena happened to fall on the feast day of St. Joseph, which I thought was pretty cool.

Not long after, someone donated a small bag of books to the Queen of Peace group. When no one else expressed interest, I took the bag and pulled out a little black book called *The Reign of Jesus through Mary*. It was full of "thee's" and "thou's" and I had no desire to decipher Old English, but for some reason I could not put this book down. Every time I did, I had to pick it up again. It was as if the book were saying, "Read me!"

Back in my unit, I opened it to the front page, which read, "Secrets of Mary. Doctrine of the Holy Slavery of Love by St. Louis de Montfort." I had never heard of St. Louis de Montfort. But somehow I knew with every fiber of my being that this was the answer to my novena. I didn't understand it, but my soul seemed to leap within me. Hairs were standing up all over my body and I became very emotional as I read the opening words "Predestined soul, I am about to share with you a secret that the Most High has taught me, which I have not been able to find in any book, old or new...Before you read any further, get down on your knees and say the Ave Maris Stella and the Veni Creator." I had never heard of these prayers, but I found them in the back of the book. Blubbering, and ignoring the fact that there were other convicts around me in the dormitory, I got down on my knees and read the prayers. I was thoroughly convinced that this came from God through St. Joseph, and I commenced to devour the book. I was on fire and determined to make the consecration it described. The book mentioned two other books, *True Devotion to Mary* and *The Imitation of Christ*. I started worrying about how I could possibly get these, but when I looked inside the bag again, I found *True Devotion* and read it on the spot. My desire to be consecrated grew even stronger.

At the following Rosary group, a new volunteer, unaware of my desire, gave me a small orange book entitled *Total Preparation for the Consecration of the Blessed Virgin Mary* by St. Louis de Montfort. It contained readings from *The Imitation of Christ*. According to the schedule in the book, the next time to start the month-long consecration was the very next day, March 26, Easter Sunday. I was consecrated to Jesus through Mary thirty-three days later, on

April 28, the feast day of St. Louis de Montfort. I figured St. Joseph must have been working overtime.

Once I made this consecration, there was no turning back. Although I did not feel worthy to be called one of Our Lady's, I desired it all the same. I had a rough time being good and had to go to Confession constantly, but I would try and do lots of little things and offer them to Our Lady. When I wanted to mouth off to another guy, I would give my mouth to our Lady, and I would automatically clam up. If I was looking too hard at one of the women who worked in the prison, I gave Our Lady my eyes. This little practice really helped me.

I also began sharing copies of Wayne Weible's newspaper with some of the other inmates. I encouraged a few of them to get together with me to pray the Rosary and live the messages of Medjugorje. One guy, Vinnie, was interested in what I had to say. He started praying the Rosary with me, under our breath and with our hands in our pockets as we walked the grounds. I talked to Father about organizing a Medjugorje prayer group but he was pretty pessimistic. He had tried to form a prayer group for the past nine years and could never find any interest.

Vinnie and I, however, were determined. There was an old school building on the prison campus and Vinnie convinced me to ask one of the guards if we could use an empty classroom to say our prayers. To my surprise, he was cooperative. Vinnie and I started that day in an empty classroom, praying all fifteen decades of the Rosary and adding three more Hail Marys in thanksgiving for the room. Within two weeks we had about fourteen guys joining us. They were gangsters, international drug dealers, murderers, bikers, and con men. We would pray the Rosary, read the readings from

Mass, and do other prayers. I kept telling the guys to pray for Our Lady's intentions, but they wanted to pray for their own needs as well. Eventually they started a "sick list" and soon the whole prison learned about it and started to petition us to pray for certain individuals. One young boy we prayed for, an inmate's son, seemed to have a miraculous healing from a hole in his heart. Our prayers were being answered.

Next I started talking the guys into going to Confession. Some of them had unconfessed murders on their hearts and they were afraid that the priest would turn them in. Gradually, they trusted him and filled up two sides of a legal-size piece of paper with every sin imaginable, with tick marks after each to account for how often these sins were committed. When someone came to Mass and received Communion who had not been there in months, we would stop him afterward and with "charity" help him to examine his conscience. We were far from saints ourselves, but Our Lady showed us that despite our flaws, she loved us because we were trying.

In August, I was sitting on my bed with a book called *The Woman,* the cover of which had a picture of Our Lady with the moon at her feet. I opened it to a part about a priest in France in 1830 who was discouraged because only a handful of people came to Mass daily. During the Consecration, he distinctly heard a voice say, *"Consecrate this parish to the Immaculate Heart of Mary."* The priest tried to shake it off. While making his thanksgiving, he heard it again. Convinced, he consecrated the parish and about four hundred people started showing up for daily Mass. Wow, I thought. Just imagine if we consecrated the prison. Maybe everyone would start praying.

I talked to Father about this idea and pointed out that the Feast of the Assumption was coming up. I told him I would even write up a consecration that he could look over. I handed out Mary Queen of Hearts novenas to everyone in the group and asked them to pray that Our Lady would give us the grace to consecrate the prison. I wrote up a prayer that consecrated everyone in all five prison units, including the employees, visitors, and delivery staff, as well as those who drove by, flew over, or came within the vicinity of the prison complex. We carried out this consecration on August 15.

Three months later, on a cold November afternoon, I looked up in the sky, as I had a habit of doing, to bless God for putting joy in my heart. This particular day the sky was a beautiful blue with only one cloud. But it wasn't an ordinary cloud—it was like a veil of cloud that covered the entire prison complex. In the middle of the cloud was a perfect circle that allowed the blue sky to show through, and at its center it looked as if someone had airbrushed a perfect dove. I thought this was pretty remarkable, but I'm not one to look for signs from God because I see it in His creation all around me. After a while, I looked up again and the perfect circle remained unaltered, with rays of light emanating from its perimeter. This time I called some of the guys to have a look. They thought it was remarkable, too. We prayed the Rosary for thirty minutes in the field and the cloud never changed until we were finished. The next day, some other guys said that earlier in the day, they saw a perfect heart in the circle that transformed into a dove. Eleven days later, Father Stefano Gobbi came to our prison and gave us a message from Our Lady. We figured she must have been pleased with our consecration.

In December that year, I was released from the New Jersey prison, but I still owed parole time to Tennessee. My intention was to serve my time (and the rest of my life) in Florida, finding some quiet space to live a humble Catholic life. That, however, was not God's plan. Word of my conversion got out and I was sought after to share my testimony at various Marian conferences throughout the country. The schedule was grueling, and I did not preserve enough personal time for the four to six hours of daily prayer I had been doing in prison, where I was completely focused on God. Father Hewett, who had foreseen my notoriety, gave me some solid advice that I unfortunately did not heed: he told me that when I got out of prison, I should try to be a reservoir and not a stream. That's because I have a tendency to try and help other people and use myself up in the process. By speaking at conferences for nearly two years, as powerful a witness as I was for those who attended, I let slip from my fingers that which was the meat of my conversion. Instead of staying focused on Jesus and Our Lady, I tried to counsel and fix people myself. It was like St. Peter in the Bible. He could walk on water as long as he was looking at the Lord, but as soon as he took his eyes off of Christ and looked at himself, he began to sink. I began to sink, too. In looking at myself, all I saw was weakness and failure, and before long I started giving in to old vices. I got myself in trouble and eventually had a nervous breakdown.

During this time, it was as though hell had opened its doors and every evil force available was trying to destroy me. Perhaps Satan was angry with me because many people, men especially, were coming back to the Church after hearing my testimony. Filled with regret and shame for the people I had hurt and let down, I tried to hide in the subculture that had always been my home, but I realized that I did not belong there. I could not abandon myself to my old life and I could not unlearn what I had learned. In these dismal places, among lost and broken people, I would speak about God's love and mercy. Even in my fall, I was called to be a witness. On December 8, 1993, I returned to prison to finish up the rest of my Tennessee sentence due to violating my parole during my breakdown. I came home finally in 1998, twenty-three years of prison life over at last.

In His infinite mercy, God provided me with a saving grace: a faith-filled wife who has seen me through my darkest hours. Today there are so many people I would like to seek forgiveness from, but I don't know where most of them are anymore and my health prohibits me from leaving my home easily. For these people I offer up my daily torment of every kind of physical, spiritual, mental, and emotional suffering imaginable. Although I can never make things right by myself, I entrust these people to Our Lady, knowing that she can bring them peace and healing.

I still hear from some of the guys who were incarcerated with me at Southern State, and many of them are leading good, Catholic lives in their new freedom. I also understand that there are a number of prayer groups still thriving at the prison, and that Medjugorje continues to bear good fruit there. The inmates are shown a video of my testimony, and they continue to pray for me and consider me a brother. While I will never take lightly the unmerited grace God granted me back in Tennessee, I have come to realize that His greatest miracle is the forgiveness of my sins. That unfailing mercy is what keeps me living another day. Father Hewett once told me that a saint is a sinner who keeps getting up. That's what I cling to, the fact that we can always pick ourselves up and start again. We can always come back and be forgiven. And that's true freedom for all of us.

Jim Jennings, Indiana

"Dear children, my call that you live the messages which I am giving you is a daily one, especially, little children, because I want to draw you closer to the heart of Jesus. Therefore, little children, I am calling you today to the prayer of consecration to Jesus, my dear Son, so that each of your hearts may be His. And then I am calling you to consecration to my immaculate heart. I want you to consecrate yourselves as individuals, families, and parishes so that all belongs to God through my hands. Therefore, dear little children, pray that you may comprehend the greatness of this message which I am giving you. I do not want anything for myself, rather, all for the salvation of your souls. Satan is strong and, therefore, you, little children, by constant prayer press tightly to my motherly heart. Thank you for having responded to my call." Message of October 25, 1988

2
Carry My Messages

Every pilgrimage to Medjugorje is full of surprises, and my June 2001 trip was no exception. On this pilgrimage, a few of the people with whom I was traveling had the unique experience of seeing something like gold dust appear on our priest's face and hair during the Corpus Christi procession. I, however, did not. Some people—most of my group, in fact—saw the sun spin. Again, I did not. Nor did I see the cross on Mt. Krizevac disappear or blaze with fire. These were all gifts to the people who experienced them, "a hug from the Blessed Mother," explained Sandee McAleer, our group leader. My special gift in Medjugorje was quite different from these, but nonetheless, just as remarkable.

My story actually began two years prior when I was in Medjugorje for the eighteenth anniversary of the apparitions. Because of the great crowd, I had to sit on a curb on the side of St. James Church for the Croatian Mass. During the Rosary afterward, an adorable little boy holding a set of rosary beads walked up to me and I took out my camera. When the photo was developed later, I knew there was something special about it. To me, this little boy seemed to be a "poster boy for the Rosary." Everyone I showed it to agreed. One woman looked at the picture and said, "Those eyes—they are the eyes of Jesus." It was as if the little boy were urging, "Please pray the Rosary with me."

A year later, I had a tote bag made up featuring this photograph with the words "Whoever does not accept the Kingdom of God like a child will not enter it." As people began to admire the bag, a thought occurred to me: Perhaps I could sell the totes in order to raise money for an orphanage. I decided to give the idea a try. The first batch sold quickly, so I placed another order. Next, I researched the Internet for the right orphanage and was overwhelmed by how many there were throughout the world. I sent out letters and e-mails with pictures of the tote bag to various organizations that supported orphanages, but to my disappointment I never heard back from any of them.

Some time later, I was reading a flyer for a Medjugorje conference in Ohio when I noticed that the profits would benefit "Hearts of the World Marian Center" for Sister Janja's orphanage in Mostar, near Medjugorje. I decided to send a note to the organization with a picture of the tote bag. A few weeks later, I received a phone call from a very excited woman who ran the Center. She loved the idea of the totes and wanted to take me up on my offer. And so I began a little ministry of selling tote bags and donating the money to Sister Janja's orphanage. Many people who purchased the totes asked me who the little boy was. I said I did not know the little boy's name or where he was from, but he was among 75,000 pilgrims in Medjugorje at the time of my visit.

Two years later, my son and I traveled to Medjugorje with Hearts of the World. One of the side trips we made was to Mostar to visit Sister Janja's orphanage and present her with our donations. Sister took one look at my tote bag and said, "That looks like little Boris." Then she did a double-take and said, "That *is* little Boris." It turns out that the child I had been calling "my poster boy for the Rosary," whose image was helping to raise money for the orphanage, had actually been an orphan under Sister's care years earlier. I burst into tears. What an awesome surprise, one that could only have been orchestrated from above! Instantly, I understood why none of the other orphanages had answered my letters—God had planned this little miracle all along.

After I composed myself, Sister Janja told me this little boy's story. He was placed in the orphanage at a young age when his mother, a single parent, became unable to care for him due to disability. Sister said that a beautiful and loving family adopted Boris a couple of years ago. She also said that she had not heard anything more about the child in years until just recently, when she was told a remarkable story. About three weeks earlier, Boris had woken up at one o'clock in the morning and had run into his parents' room in tears. When his mother asked him what was wrong, he said between sobs that he had dreamed she had died. The mother hugged her son and assured him that she was just fine, letting him sleep the rest of the night between her and her husband. At eight o'clock the next morning, Boris's mother got a call from a woman at the social services office in Central Bosnia. She called to say that Boris's biological mother had passed away in the night. When Boris's adoptive mother inquired about the time of death, the woman answered, "About one in the morning." Needless to say, I was speechless.

I feel so blessed to have been gifted with the photo of this little angel. For the past few years, I have sold many tote bags, raising a substantial amount of money for the orphanage. I often carry my little tote bag as a quiet but effective way to promote Our Lady's call to prayer. But now God calls me to carry on a new ministry.

Today I am the editor of *The Spirit of Medjugorje* newsletter, a monthly publication distributed to more than fifty states and thirty-three foreign countries. My involvement with the newsletter is no less of a miracle than the story of Boris. During my first pilgrimage to Medjugorje in 1998, a stranger approached me during one of the visionary's talks and commented that, as a teacher, I should be taking notes. I did not know this man, or how he knew I was a teacher, but from that point on, I was careful to take copious notes. When I returned home, a woman from church who was listening to my stories about the trip handed me a copy of *The Spirit of Medjugorje* newsletter and suggested I submit to them. Although I was not a professional writer, I followed this woman's advice. The editor, Joan Wieszczyk, liked what I had written and published all my articles over the following year, after which she invited me to continue writing for the newsletter.

At the 2000 Medjugorje conference in Notre Dame, Joan asked me a surprising question. If anything were to happen to her, she wanted to know, would I be willing to take over the newsletter? I told Joan I would pray about it for a few days. When I recalled Our Lady's message of June 5, 1986, *"I wish you to be active in living and spreading the messages,"* I knew I could not refuse. Besides, in the two years I had known Joan, she was never sick, not even with a cold. But then it happened. Two years later, Joan suffered a heart attack and the newsletter was suddenly thrown in my lap. Joan had made me a co-editor some time before, but my primary job was proofreading. Now I needed to do the writing, the layout, everything! I implored Our Lady for help. Much of the summer was spent learning how to set up the newsletter and keep the books. Joan eventually had surgery and made a pilgrimage of thanksgiving to Medjugorje, where she prayed about her retirement. When she returned, she asked me to take over as editor.

It has been both exhilarating and at times overwhelming to take on this special ministry in addition to my job as a math teacher, but the rewards have been bountiful. When I'm feeling stressed, I take comfort and courage in Joan's following words: "This is Our Lady's newsletter. We are just the instruments to bring it to the public." Each month, the right stories come in just when I need them, and the newsletter makes its deadline. In the seventeen years that *The Spirit of Medjugorje* has been published, we have never required a subscription rate; we exist solely on free will offerings. Our Lady always provides and we, in turn, inspire people to live and spread her messages. Recently, I've gathered some of the most compelling stories in a book called *The Best of The Spirit of Medjugorje* and the latest project I am considering is putting the newsletters on cassette tapes and CDs for people who cannot see well enough to read. If this additional ministry is the will of Our Lord and Our Lady, it, too, will be carried out.

June Klins, Pennsylvania

"Dear children! Today I invite you to conversion. This is the most important message that I have given you here. Little children, I wish that each of you become a carrier of my messages. I invite you, little children, to live the messages that I have given you over these years. This time is a time of grace. Especially now, when the Church is inviting you to prayer and conversion, I also, little children, invite you to live my messages that I have given you during the time since I appear here. Thank you for having responded to my call."

Message of February 25, 1996

3

Illuminate All Souls

My conversion began in 2001, at a time when my spiritual life was in ruins. I was twenty-one years old, still basking in the so-called "college experience" of drinking excessively and taking everything in life for granted. Most of my Sundays were spent nursing hangovers, and Easter for me was nothing more than a time for spring break and beach parties. School itself had been good to me: after receiving a writing scholarship to attend the University of Tampa, I won an array of creative writing, screenwriting, and filmmaking awards. In those days, however, most of my creative output was replete with cynicism and a denial of Christian thinking.

Although a baptized Roman Catholic, I had not set foot in a church for over a decade. In fact, I despised the idea of giving up part of a weekend for something about which I was unsure. Yes, I believed in God, but years before a group of young fundamentalist Christians that shared lockers near mine in high school had driven me away from Christianity. I would hear them talk about how other religions were purely evil, how Christ would never accept a non-Christian person. They cursed people like Ahmed, the gentle Muslim boy from Saudi Arabia, and Jacob, a soft-spoken Jewish boy who proudly wore his Star of David on a chain. They cursed everyone who did not share their beliefs. Their prejudiced words, which I mistakenly took as representative of all Christians, gave me a sour taste for the whole religion.

By the grace of God, my jaded view of Christianity was about to change when my mother called me one summer with a strange proposal. I'll never forget her words: "Will you come with me to Bosnia?" "Sure," I said jokingly. "Let me pack my bags." I was surprised to learn that my mother was serious. There was a trip going to Medjugorje in less than a week and there were a few open spots. Only six months before, she had gone to Medjugorje on a pilgrimage. Her journey back to religion is fascinating itself.

My mother's unusual calling began one day at a Florida antique store when she purchased several books written in German about the Third Reich and Nazi Germany. At the time, my mom—twice-divorced and looking for answers—was immersed in the New Age movement. After a series of dreams and past-life regressions, she held the notion that she had been reincarnated from the soul of a dead German man. The books looked attractively old to her and she thought these would make good additions to her antique bookshelf.

The night she brought the books home, strange things started to happen. The first instance occurred while she was reading in her bedroom. She heard what sounded like the garbled voice of a child emanating from the living room, followed by the sound of her dog, a female Labrador, growling and barking. My mom rushed out of her room to find the dog in the middle of the living room, its back bristling in fear, cowering and growling at nothing. That night, my mother was awakened by the sound of her bedroom door creaking. No windows were open and the dogs were in their pens. She finally went back to sleep, but was repeatedly awakened to the sound of the door creaking, and each time the door was cocked at a different angle.

I was in Alaska that summer working as a fishing guide and I remember calling my mother almost every day to find out what ghostly event had occurred the night before. The haunting seemed to be growing in intensity. My mother began to suffer from nightmares in which she dreamed that demonic beings were chasing her. She continued to see strange images throughout the house that would disappear or meld into shadow and the television set kept turning on by itself to a cartoon channel. At the advice of her parents, she finally called a local Catholic priest named Father Rick. He walked through the house dispersing blessings and holy water while my mother told him about the events.

"Has anyone died in this house?" Father Rick asked her. "No," my mother replied. "It's a brand new house and I'm the first person to live here." "Have you recently brought anything into the house?" My mom turned to the bookshelf and pointed. "Just these old books." Father Rick approached the books cautiously and sprinkled them with holy water. "I don't even want to touch these," he said. "Get them out of here immediately." My mother got rid of the books and that was the last she heard of the restless spirit, but one thing remained: her new fascination with Catholicism. After all, she had seen the power of Christ in her own home. Father Rick invited her to visit Medjugorje and her first experience there brought her back into the Church, even to the point of becoming a eucharistic minister.*

Therefore, when my mother invited me to Medjugorje on her second pilgrimage, I promptly agreed. Within a week

---

* Throughout these pages are references to "eucharistic ministers." The proper term, as of the printing of the book, is "extraordinary minister of the Eucharist." The popular term has been retained because of the informal nature of the testimonies.

I was soaring high above the Atlantic with a group of people I had never met before. My seat was right beside Father Rick and we talked for the entire flight. I had heard the story many times about what was supposedly happening in Medjugorje, but as a journalist-in-the-making, I was skeptical. It would take hard evidence to convince me that the events in Medjugorje were real.

On my first afternoon there, I attended Mass at St. James Church. I listened to the priest, trying to recall when I had last been to church. I had to watch what other people were doing and imitate them so as not to stand out. My unease was heightened when I had to remain at the pew while everyone else moved solemnly to receive Christ in the Eucharist.

Later, I sat alone in the churchyard and stared up at Cross Mountain as the sun sank low on the horizon, setting the hills ablaze. Had I made a mistake by coming here? I didn't seem to fit in with the crowd. I believed in God, but I was hard-set against organized religion because I did not understand it. My place of worship had always been the wilderness, as a fishing guide and outdoorsman. Immersing myself in nature was how I learned the value of patience and contemplation, not in a church pew being addressed by a priest.

And so I decided to experience Medjugorje the way I knew best. I left a note telling my mother not to worry, that I had gone to climb Cross Mountain alone and would be back by sunrise. I walked through the narrow streets as children and old women stared at me from open windows. It felt good to be alone in such a foreign world, surrounded by the trappings of a different culture. A few chickens followed me until I got to the base of Mt. Krizevac. An elderly woman had just ambled down the mountain, and I noticed that she was barefoot. I asked her if she had climbed the entire way like that. "Peccato," she said in Italian, smiling. And then, in English, she whispered, "For my sins."

Staring up at the far-off peak, I removed my shoes and put them in my backpack. I had heard that climbing the mountain barefoot was a good way to be eased of the burdens of one's sins, and if an old woman could do it, then I would have to try. The worn path was a painful combination of sharp, gray rocks and briar-laced vines. At different intervals along the climb, I stopped to meditate at the large bronze Stations of the Cross as I rested my aching feet. I prayed that I might be granted some sort of sign that the Medjugorje phenomenon was real.

The sun had nearly set and the mountain was bathed in pinkish light as I trudged along a straightaway in the trail. Up ahead I could see the third Station of the Cross. As I had been doing for nearly the entire climb, I glanced down to watch my step and then looked up again to be sure I was walking in the right direction. It was then that I saw a figure turning the corner just fifteen feet away, coming toward me. He was dressed in a white priest's robe like the one worn at Mass, and he had an enormous rosary around his neck.

I glanced quickly again at my feet, wondering why a priest would be dressed like that on top of the mountain. When I looked up again for the strange man, he was gone. He had vanished right in front of me. An overwhelming feeling of awe and wonder rushed through me as I ran to the spot where he had been standing just seconds before. I even looked in the nearby briars to see if he might be hiding, but I was completely alone.

Although I realized I had just seen an apparition, I did not feel alarmed. This was not at all like the spirits my mother had encountered at home. Beaming with happiness,

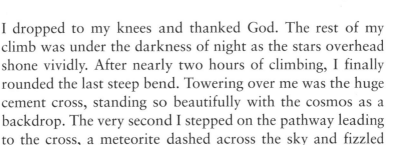

I dropped to my knees and thanked God. The rest of my climb was under the darkness of night as the stars overhead shone vividly. After nearly two hours of climbing, I finally rounded the last steep bend. Towering over me was the huge cement cross, standing so beautifully with the cosmos as a backdrop. The very second I stepped on the pathway leading to the cross, a meteorite dashed across the sky and fizzled out behind the cross. I made my way to the altar and sat on the cool cement, peering down at the lights of Medjugorje far below. I took out a rosary my mother had given me, along with a pamphlet that explained how to use it. After seeing the vision of that priest earlier, I vowed to learn this prayer. I used my flashlight to read while I clenched each tiny bead and recited the prayers, offering them for my family, friends, and even for those who had wronged me in the past.

Before my pilgrimage was over, I had the chance to hear Father Jozo Zovko speak in Siroki Brijeg. Father Jozo was the pastor at Medjugorje in the early years of the apparitions and had been imprisoned by the communist Yugoslavian government. He still bore the scars of his torture and yet he was the most peaceful-looking man I had ever seen. After the talk, Father Rick joined the other priests to be prayed over by him and then they in turn prayed over the pilgrims. People began collapsing all over the place and my first thought was that they were faking. Soon Father Rick made his way to where my mother and I were standing. He began to pray over her and I watched in disbelief as she, too, fell down. When he stood in front of me and placed his hands over my forehead, it felt as if an electrical current was surging through my veins. My knees grew weak and soon I could no longer feel my arms as the most pleasant warmth overtook me. But I fought this feeling because I did not want to fall down, and somehow I was able to regain my senses. As Father Rick moved to the next person, he caught me off guard and again raised his hand over me. This time peace swept over me like warm water. I realized two people behind me were lowering me to the ground. I clenched onto some inner strength and stood up before my body even touched the floor. In retrospect, I regret not allowing myself to be overtaken by this strange bliss.

I left Medjugorje determined not only to change my life, but to help spread the messages so that others could benefit as well. Knowing that many people my age would not invest the time to read a book about the apparitions, I decided to create an hour-long video. Before Medjugorje, I had planned to go to Hollywood and try to make it in the film industry, but now my conversion called me to do something much greater. After graduating from college in May of 2001, I went to work preparing for this production. I needed over $3,000 to buy the right video equipment, so I decided to fast and pray, since Our Lady said this could stop wars and change the laws of nature. In answer to my prayers, my grandmother felt compelled to help me purchase what I needed, and I was on my way to Medjugorje again, just after the twentieth anniversary of the apparitions.

This time I would be staying with Jakov, the youngest visionary, in the small guest quarters attached to his house. Jakov's shyness was evident, but beneath it all I could see wisdom far beyond his years. He agreed to let me interview him, and one of his comments helped me see a more tolerant side of Christianity. "Our Lady is calling everyone to conversion, not just Catholics," he told me. "The messages that Our Lady is giving here in Medjugorje are for the whole world, for all humanity. Our Lady always comes as a mother. She is a mother to all." By the end of the pilgrimage,

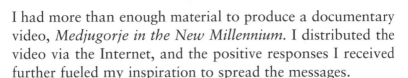

I had more than enough material to produce a documentary video, *Medjugorje in the New Millennium*. I distributed the video via the Internet, and the positive responses I received further fueled my inspiration to spread the messages.

Back home in Florida, I realized that my spiritual life had changed dramatically. I no longer cared about the sinful life I had once led. Peace was all I sought. Prayer had become part of my daily routine, a new kind of praying that had previously been foreign to me—prayer from the heart, as Jakov had described it—and I worked hard to follow the messages of Medjugorje. My experiences helped change my mind about a lot of things, including marriage and commitment, and I proposed to my longtime girlfriend, Lisa, with a simple prayer: "God, please let her say yes!"

After the successful release of my first documentary video, I embarked on a second to compare Medjugorje to other Marian apparitions. Traveling to Lourdes, Garabandal, and Fatima, and then to Medjugorje to stay with the visionary Ivan, the result was a documentary called *The Fruits of Mary*. During this pilgrimage, I fulfilled what I felt was a milestone in my conversion: I became part of the Church. I started by giving my general confession to a young priest who was kind enough to have patience with me while I sniveled my way through the sacrament. But when it was over, I felt completely free. Soon after, I received Holy Communion for the first time.

On a fourth visit to Medjugorje in May 2004, I was accompanied by my fiancée, Lisa, and stayed with the visionary Mirjana. During an on-camera interview, Mirjana explained the special mission with which Our Lady has entrusted her. "The Blessed Mother comes to me so that we may pray together for unbelievers. She doesn't call them unbelievers, but rather those who have not yet felt the love of God. Those of us who already believe can change them, but only with our prayers and with our example."

This message really hit me. Lisa had been raised without religion, yet she was the nicest, most honest person I had ever known. Still, it was difficult for me to live my new faith with her as an outsider. I truly wanted Lisa to witness the benefits of my faith, so I prayed that she might see the light. That evening, she did—literally—during one of Ivan's nighttime apparitions on Mt. Podbrdo. As people bowed their heads in prayer, Lisa saw a strange ball of light glide overhead and disappear into the brush on the hillside. She saw it a second time, coming down the hillside toward the crowd and approaching Ivan. It pulsed brightly three times before vanishing, and then Ivan went into ecstasy. The experience helped make Lisa a believer.

Currently, I have a third video in production. My hope is to make a documentary about Medjugorje that has the power to convert people just by watching it. I'm using everything I've learned in filmmaking to put it together and the History Channel has already expressed interest in airing some of my footage in a program called "Visions of Mary." I am entrusting this project completely to our Blessed Mother, that it may open the eyes and hearts of those who do not yet believe, that they may see the love of the Father as she has so lovingly shown it to me.

Sean Bloomfield, Florida

"Dear children, pray for your brothers who haven't experienced the love of the Father, for those whose only importance is life on earth. Open your hearts towards them and see in them my Son, who loves them. Be my light and illuminate all souls where darkness reigns. Thank you for having responded to my call." Message of March 2, 1997

4
Fast with the Heart

To write about fasting almost seems as if it would negate the fast itself, because, according to scripture, fasting should be done in private for only God to know. To talk about fasting is to reveal the weakness in my heart and soul, to reveal the timidity of my will, but I do it in the hopes of helping others to embrace the gift of this discipline.

The first news of Medjugorje came to me from a friend who told me that teenagers in Yugoslavia were seeing the Blessed Mother every day. As with the blackout in New York City, or the day President Kennedy was shot, I can remember exactly where I was and what I was doing when I first heard of Medjugorje. It was 1990, and I was battling alcoholism. Overwhelmed by despair, and after numerous hospitalizations for depression and suicide attempts, I received my diagnosis: post–traumatic stress disorder, chronic, delayed. My husband was desperately trying to run our family business and take care of our four young children. I, on the other hand, was functioning on a very basic level, making some meals and getting the kids off to school, but sadly, I was not emotionally available to anyone.

The news about the Blessed Mother appearing in Yugoslavia took a minute to be absorbed into my emotionally numb brain. When it actually dawned on me, my heart started pounding and I felt a rush of adrenaline as I contemplated something of the magnitude of Fatima or Lourdes happening in my lifetime. I went home and found the rosary beads my mother had given me for my eleventh birthday. Memories returned of the family Rosary and of being consecrated to the Blessed Mother in eighth grade. Looking back now, I realize that despite the darkness in which I had been living, a spark of hope was kept alive through those rediscovered rosary beads. I would also go to Mass and do what I called "Bible roulette," that is, opening the Bible to see what God had to say to me; usually I did this when I was most desperate. Still unfamiliar with the call of the Blessed Mother to fasting, I nonetheless engaged in abstaining from alcohol, my drug of choice, each day. Fighting suicidal thoughts, however, was my biggest battle. Without alcohol, I had nothing to deaden the pain within, and the deep, raw, emotional wounds intensified to the point that the thought of dying gave me a false sense of control over my life.

To the best of my understanding, my life seemed to have plummeted into a spiraling bottomless depression three years prior, in 1987, a year after the birth of our fourth child. At the time I was helping in the sacramental preparation for my oldest son, Matthew. On the night he made his First Reconciliation, Matthew returned from the priest and said to me, "Your turn, Mom." It had been six years since I had gone to Confession, and the last experience had not been a pleasant one. With four beautiful children and a loving husband, I had much to be grateful for, but tears were always close to the surface and such was the case that night. I told the priest that I knew I had sinned, but I could not pinpoint any. Then I burst into tears. At this point he offered me an opportunity for spiritual direction, to which I agreed.

Meetings were weekly, usually in the rectory. As we began touching on deeper issues that I had avoided for years,

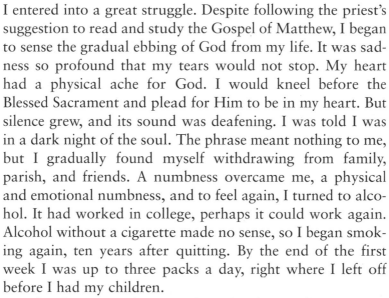

I entered into a great struggle. Despite following the priest's suggestion to read and study the Gospel of Matthew, I began to sense the gradual ebbing of God from my life. It was sadness so profound that my tears would not stop. My heart had a physical ache for God. I would kneel before the Blessed Sacrament and plead for Him to be in my heart. But silence grew, and its sound was deafening. I was told I was in a dark night of the soul. The phrase meant nothing to me, but I gradually found myself withdrawing from family, parish, and friends. A numbness overcame me, a physical and emotional numbness, and to feel again, I turned to alcohol. It had worked in college, perhaps it could work again. Alcohol without a cigarette made no sense, so I began smoking again, ten years after quitting. By the end of the first week I was up to three packs a day, right where I left off before I had my children.

The depression became clinical; I lost well over forty pounds in five months. At five foot ten I was down to 128 pounds, and death began to beckon its bony finger at me. The pain was not physical, not emotional, but spiritual, and it hurt worse than any broken bone I'd ever had. The difference was, I could not point to a place and say, "This hurts, please fix it." In August I struggled with suicidal thoughts. I took a bottle of pills and poured them down the toilet, taking only two and climbing into bed. The two were enough to send me to the hospital for the first time, unconscious, due to my physical deterioration. I spent three weeks being rehydrated and fed, and was counseled by a therapist before discharge. However, I had nothing to say to this man. Week after week, I had no desire to replay what little of my childhood I could remember. He asked me to tell him about my earliest memory, and I could remember only two things. The first was my fifth birthday party where my mother gave me a scapular that I would wear every day of my life. The second memory was of my First Holy Communion and the immense joy and unity I felt with Jesus, to the point of tears. I did not understand why no one else was crying around me, and so I hid my tears, not wanting to be laughed at.

On December 3, 1987, I attempted suicide again, only to be transported by ambulance to the emergency room, where my heart stopped. I was admitted to the intensive care unit and came out of a coma the next day.

Our Blessed Mother must have heard my feeble attempts at praying the Rosary and never left my side, because somehow I survived this dark period of my life. I began the long climb upward, prayer by prayer, clinging to that rosary like a lifeline. In December 1997, a series of events had transpired that enabled me to travel to Medjugorje by myself. My prayer during that first pilgrimage was not that I would receive great signs like others had, but rather that a complete healing would take place in my heart, body, emotions, and mind. I longed to be totally cleansed of all sadness, resentment, guilt, regret, and sin. I also prayed that I would be given graces to continue praying and fasting with my heart when I returned home. Fasting is something I had tried before my pilgrimage to Medjugorje, but I had failed miserably. There I hoped to receive the gift of fasting. I came to understand that fasting is a great gift to return to the Blessed Mother and I wanted to shower her with gifts for her ceaseless love.

My pilgrimage was a great boost to my spirituality. I was able to pray for three hours a day, saying two Rosaries in the morning and one in the afternoon. I attended Mass daily and read the Bible and other readings of the Church. For the first time that I could remember, my heart was like a song. As with all prayer of the heart, things began to happen. Confession became necessary every two weeks as God gently began to reveal to me the sins buried under rationalization and years of delusional thinking.

By the end of 2001, I was exhausted from my job and from various family crises. Someone suggested that I try a retreat. I had heard that Father Jozo conducted an excellent one in Siroki Brijeg, a few hours from Medjugorje, so I made arrangements to go. While the entire week was powerful, the critical points for me were the meditations on the mysteries of the Rosary read by Father Jozo during each hour of adoration. The words brought us into the scene of each mystery, and for me, the sorrowful mysteries were particularly poignant: the betrayal of Jesus by a close friend and apostle, the selling of Jesus for money, the kiss that was a lie. These thoughts careened in my head, striking one nerve after another. Memories flooded into my mind between the erratic thoughts of family, work, prayer, food, fear, and desire. The kiss of betrayal slathered on my mouth, *on my soul,* by an alcoholic priest...not one priest, but three of them. These issues had been talked about and faced through years of therapy and years of torment. But the root resentment had not been identified until Father Jozo's reading of the Agony in the Garden. I had been robbed of my innocence. But also stolen from me was a desire, nurtured through childhood and into my teen years, to enter an order of sisters who spent their days in prayer. This, I now realized, was at the heart of my disconnected thoughts when I would go to retreats or pilgrimages to sit in silence with God and contemplate his immense goodness and love. And the knowledge of this caused a flood of tears that would not stop. But they were not tears of self-pity; they were my offering for the souls of those priests, for their forgiveness and for God's mercy on them.

In so many confessions back home, I did not feel God's forgiveness. During that retreat I promptly went to Confession with new hope. I knocked, and a voice welcomed me in. I blurted out all that had occurred on the retreat, including my past so that the priest would have a framework of my history. The tears flooded, and he came close to me and put his hand on my head. It was the first time a priest had done that where I felt safe; in the past I would have slapped that hand away. The priest introduced himself as Father Ciarin, an exorcist from Ireland, and he said that it was no coincidence that I happened upon his confessional. Some of the torment I shared with him that had started back in 1987 included a sensation of being plagued by evil spirits. I would lie awake at night and watch ugly creatures, not quite human and not quite animal, slither into my bedroom or move past my door. They were present whether my eyes were open or shut, causing me sleepless nights and the terrifying fear that I was going crazy. Father Ciarin had to leave to serve at Mass, but he told me to meet him the following afternoon in Medjugorje and he would pray over me the prayers of deliverance.

Before I left Siroki Brijeg, Father Jozo prayed over me for several minutes in front of the tabernacle in the church. The next day Father Ciarin prayed over me the Latin prayers of blessing. That evening at Mass, I was relieved that my ordeal was over and that I could bring myself to Jesus completely for healing. We were blessed the next morning to be brought into Vicka's old bedroom where her apparitions had occurred. She came in and prayed over each of us for a long time. It was a great grace, and as I left her, I felt as though I were floating.

The healing was complete. The ghosts have not returned and my soul has been freed from the spirits of darkness. Depression has left me and even during the long Vermont winters, it has not returned. The Gospel says that if a spirit is driven out, prayer and fasting is necessary so that it does not return. I have been through a range of fasting attempts, both successes and failures. Actually, I prefer to consider the latter category as times of learning. During these times I discover my sinfulness. I recognize what my heart is attached to: caffeine, sweets, salty foods, and so on, and I learn how this kind of attachment can actually become greater than my ability to love God with my whole being. Through detachment, I gain freedom.

My commitment to fasting would not be present if prayer was not primary in my life. Without prayer, fasting is an exercise focused on self. Without prayer, there is no conversation, no dialogue, and no ability to empty oneself completely into the heart of God. Fasting and prayer are great weapons given to me to cut through the lies of our culture and discover God's truth. In fasting, the truth about myself is revealed as well. It's not surprising, therefore, that great lines for confession began in Medjugorje when the Blessed Mother asked the parish to fast.

Jesus prayed and fasted, and if I am to become like Him, I must do the same. He emptied Himself for three years, and then gave Himself in the Eucharist for all time before being totally consumed on the cross by unselfish love for us. Like the wheat that is ground to make the eucharistic bread, each piece of bread I consume reminds me that I am called to be bread for others and that I must die a little to myself each day. When I thirst on fast days, I recall the last drops of water that came from Jesus' side—that great mercy poured out for us—and I ask myself: how am I mercy for others?

I find that Confession naturally flows from fasting. It is necessary to acknowledge those things I choose over God's love each day, things that become fully revealed during strict fast days. Of late it has become important to have a regular confessor who can begin to see the larger picture for me. This allows me to not only look more carefully at my sins of commission, but also those brought on by omission and indifference. Then I can work on changing the root causes of those behaviors.

The fact that I am alive and not dead, the fact that I am able to forgive and to accept forgiveness, the fact that I have desire to pray and fast and read God's Word: these are sources of great love and strength and gratitude that I cannot keep to myself. I must give away the joy I have received in order to keep it. I do this through service as an extraordinary minister of the Eucharist, a catechist for Confirmation, a volunteer in youth ministry, and a presenter for middle-school retreats.

Like the Rosary, my life has been a connection of joyful, sorrowful, glorious, and even luminous mysteries. What I count on today as reliably as my childhood rosary is the love and mercy of God and the Blessed Mother that I experience when I pray and fast with the heart.

Peggy Angstadt, Vermont

"Dear children! Also today I am with you in a special way contemplating and living the passion of Jesus in my heart. Little children, open your hearts and give me everything that

is in them: joys, sorrows and each, even the smallest, pain, that I may offer them to Jesus; so that with His immeasurable love, He may burn and transform your sorrows into the joy of His resurrection. That is why, I now call you in a special way, little children, for your hearts to open to prayer, so that through prayer you may become friends of Jesus. Thank you for having responded to my call."

Message of February 25, 1999

Eucharist

*"You do not celebrate the
Eucharist as you should. If you
would know what grace, and what gifts
you receive, you would prepare yourselves
for it each day, for an hour at least..."*
Early Message of
Our Lady, 1985

5

From Hell to Heaven

In 1992, after reaching rock bottom, I had a profound conversion experience that changed my life dramatically. Up until that point, I had gone through all a troubled teenager could, from drug abuse to grand theft. It began in Virginia Beach, where my stepfather was based in the military, and it worsened when our family moved to California. I was into drugs, sex, smoking, and drinking all by the age of eleven and things were escalating to the point of getting completely out of control. Our family moved again, outside of Los Angeles, and then across the ocean to Japan. Being uprooted continuously from my friends and my environment, I decided in my anger to teach my parents a lesson, and as soon as we got to Japan, I became an absolute living hell for them. I got involved with the wrong crowd and started doing dangerous quantities of drugs: opium, heroin, and alcohol every day, even inhaling the fumes of gasoline.

Having no concern for anything or anybody, I ran away from the military base and fled, traveling throughout the foreign country, committing felonies like stealing money, cars, and mopeds, even getting involved in running errands for the Japanese Mafia. The police finally tapped the phones to the military base and I was apprehended. I was fifteen, with long hair and a profane mouth, and was brazen enough to spit in the face of one of the military cops. I was so wild that I was shackled like an animal and deported.

My mother, understandably, suffered a great deal during this time. My actions drove her to consult with a priest out of desperation and through this process, she eventually became Catholic. She, too, was forced to leave Japan and return to the United States owing to my criminal behavior. Back home, I told my mother that I hated her, but at the same time I followed her suggestion to enter a rehabilitation center. Still, I was not ready to change. I ran away from there, too, and went back to drugs on an even greater scale. Things went from bad to worse and soon I ended up in jail in Louisiana.

My life was an absolute mess. A tattooed drop-out with hair down to my belt, I had a second failed attempt at rehabilitation and the drug use got even heavier. Then, one night in 1992, I had this sudden, peculiar, and powerful intuition that my life was about to change radically, that something was about to happen. It was a feeling so overwhelming that I turned down calls from friends to come out and party as I was accustomed to doing. I still can't explain exactly what brought about this feeling. Perhaps it was the prayers of a mother…

For a while, I remained in my bedroom waiting for this "something" to happen, and then I wandered into the hall looking for a magazine or book to read to pass the time. I searched for a magazine with pictures, like *National Geographic*, as I was not much of a reader, but I felt guided by a strong feeling to pick up a book that caught my eye. The title was *The Queen of Peace Visits Medjugorje*, a book by Father Joseph A. Pelletier. I could not seem to make out what the book was about—the words were like a foreign language to me. Looking at the pictures, I saw six children on their knees, staring up in the air. The caption said the chil-

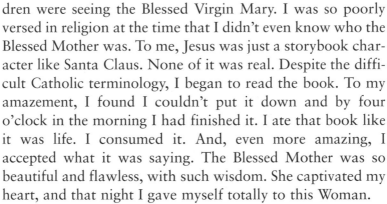

dren were seeing the Blessed Virgin Mary. I was so poorly versed in religion at the time that I didn't even know who the Blessed Mother was. To me, Jesus was just a storybook character like Santa Claus. None of it was real. Despite the difficult Catholic terminology, I began to read the book. To my amazement, I found I couldn't put it down and by four o'clock in the morning I had finished it. I ate that book like it was life. I consumed it. And, even more amazing, I accepted what it was saying. The Blessed Mother was so beautiful and flawless, with such wisdom. She captivated my heart, and that night I gave myself totally to this Woman.

The next morning I went to my mother and told her that I wanted to see a priest. She, of course, was totally shocked, seeing that I was dead serious. Frantically, she began making calls. When she couldn't find a priest who could see me that morning, we remembered there was a chaplain on the military base where we were living. My mother told me to run and find him quickly, and I dashed across the base with my long hair flowing behind me as marines with shaved heads marched past.

My story blew the Navy chaplain away. He told me to meet him at the church and sit in the back while he said Mass, and we could talk more afterward. I did as I was told. Interestingly, the name of the church was Our Lady of Victories. It was the first time I had entered a Catholic church and I sat apprehensively in the back row, waiting and watching as a small group of Filipino women recited a set of repetitious prayers that I would later discover was the Rosary. What happened next would change my life. The priest came out wearing his vestments. I had no idea what was going on—I thought perhaps there was going to be some kind of performance or something. Never having been to

Mass before, I was fascinated to watch the ladies in front of me kneel, stand, sit, and pray in unison.

At the moment of Consecration, God granted me an amazing favor. I, a twenty-year-old, drug-abusing runaway, with no previous religious education, was suddenly graced with complete understanding of what was transpiring before me. I recognized this sacred moment as a re-presentation of what had taken place two thousand years ago on Calvary, and that the Body and Blood of Christ were being poured out for me now. Time seemed to cease at that moment and I found myself at the foot of the cross with the faithful, beholding the sacrifice of the Lamb. Everything about this moment enraptured me.

By the end of Mass and my animated conversation with the Navy chaplain afterward, I was madly in love with Our Savior and ready to go door-to-door to tell everyone about it. I went home and grabbed several big black trash bags, tearing down all of my posters and throwing away just about everything in my room. I replaced it all with a picture of the pope and another of the Sacred Heart of Jesus, which the priest had given to me along with a crucifix.

I don't remember ever having said a prayer in my life before that point, but I now desired to pray with all my heart. I looked at the picture in the book of the six children on their knees with their hands folded, and I imitated this gesture. I had no idea how this all worked or what was supposed to happen next. I allowed my eyes to focus on the picture of the Sacred Heart. As I looked at that image, something within me understood with strange familiarity that this was the God-Man who died for me, and that the messages of the Blessed Virgin Mary were meant to call the world—especially people like me—to her Son.

With that, I cried profusely. You could have filled a bucket with my tears. I was so remorseful for all the things I had done that it was like every drop of fluid in my body was coming out of my eyes. Yet at the same time I knew there was hope, and I was crying tears of joy. In fact, I was practically laughing. I knew that this Jesus who had died for me really loved me and had loved me all along. My tears of repentance washed me and I remained in that position for hours.

When I finally arose, I felt peaceful, but exhausted. I lay down on the bed and, for the first time in years, I felt free. An unbelievable peace came over me. As I was on the verge of sleep, however, I was jolted awake. It was as if someone or something came from behind and knocked me "out of my body." It felt as if my soul or spirit was actually leaving me. Was I dying? I couldn't say anything; I couldn't move. I was terrorized with fear. The only person I knew to cry out to in my distress was Mary, and I cried out spiritually, screaming with everything I had, *"Ma-a-r-r-r-y!"* It was a deep cry that seemed to go on forever. All at once I felt as if I was being pushed back into my body with the force of the universe and I heard the most beautiful feminine voice I have ever heard (and will ever hear) say, *"Donnie, I am so happy."*

No one ever called me "Donnie" but my mother. It was so personal, so unbelievable. I sat up, literally a new person. I realized that I had instantly lost my craving for all my previous vices, from impure thoughts about women to cigarettes and drugs. There was no more desire to have anything to do with the lifestyle I had been living before. God had completely converted me. Christ just overwhelmed me with His love. I started "living" in the church, saying the Stations of the Cross until I was worn out to the point of sleeping on the pews. I began reciting the Rosary, wearing a scapular, and reading everything I could on the saints.

Looking back, I believe I experienced a supernatural infusion of knowledge about the faith. Within nine months, I entered the Church. Shortly after, I applied to and was accepted by the Marians of the Immaculate Conception, a small order of priests dedicated to the Divine Mercy. But first I had to go back to school. They sent me to Franciscan University of Steubenville, where I worked hard to earn a double-major bachelor's degree, graduating magna cum laude. Next I attended seminary at the Dominican House of Studies in Washington, DC, where I earned a master's degree in divinity, also graduating magna cum laude. In seminary, I was delighted to discover that most of my peers had been to or had heard about Medjugorje and they were knowledgeable about other current apparitions as well. These young men, like me, were believers, and it was exciting to realize that we were the ones who would be going out to the parishes and to the seminaries to teach. We were tomorrow's Church. It appeared to me that Our Lady was building up a sort of army, priest by priest. Each year, these special men emerge from the seminaries to take their rightful places in the world. There is a whole generation of priests coming, led by the example of the Holy Father—a generation of men who are strongly devoted to the Mother of God.

During my first year of ordination, I made a trip to Medjugorje to give thanks for my conversion and for my priesthood. I loved every minute of my pilgrimage and was particularly honored to deliver the homily as forty other priests joined me on the altar at St. James Church. To me, Medjugorje is like the edge of heaven.

The Blessed Mother remains a pillar in my priesthood today. You could say that my priesthood is very Marian at its core. It has been defined initially by my conversion experience through Medjugorje and the messages of these apparitions and others like it, through prayerful contemplation of the Rosary, and by the example of the late Pope John Paul II, who continues to serve as a primary role model for me in my vocational journey.

I truly believe that it has always been God's plan that every man needs a woman to be complete—even the God-Man Himself. He created Our Lady intentionally so that she could be there for Him, loving Him and supporting Him. I feel that in my sharing in the priesthood of Christ, Mary is a necessary part of my priesthood, too. I turn to her constantly as the feminine complement to my manhood, to be nourished spiritually by her affection and her love. She wants to hear my voice in prayer and knowing that she wants to be with me really sustains me in an age that is very trying for men entering the priesthood.

I find that in having an intense relationship of devotion and piety with the Blessed Virgin, I can experience the fullness of priesthood. I've seen a lot of men who have fallen away from their vocations and one of the recurring problems is that they did not have a deep relationship with the Blessed Virgin Mary. This is very unfortunate. The good news, however, is that a large majority of the men in seminaries today do have a strong devotion to Our Lady. Many people refer to the Virgin as "Our Mother" and rightfully so, because certainly she is that for all of us. But for men, there is something special about the title "Our Lady." She is our Queen and she inspires us to want to do battle for her. There's something almost knightly about this new generation of priests who have been touched by Medjugorje and by the example of our Holy Father.

It seems that the twentieth century has brought about a renewal of a certain brand of Marian devotion that is very chivalrous. Movements have started, like *Militia of the Immaculata,* inspired by the example of Maximilian Kolbe, and like *The Legion of Mary,* founded by lay person Frank Duff, who is currently being considered for beatification. I çan identify with the image of the Blessed Mother that these movements foster. Mary is the beauty in my life that is worth defending and worth dying for. Every man needs someone beautiful in his life for whom he is willing to lay down his life. Christ did that for the Church and for Our Lady; they are really two sides of the same coin. Our Lady, as the saints say, is basically the blueprint of the Church. You can't really love one without loving the other. When I love Our Lady, I have the assurance that I am loving the Church as Jesus desires. From my experience, if priests do not have a proper understanding of Mary and her significance for their priesthood, their understanding of what the Church is will probably be slightly off as well. They won't be willing to defend, love, or die for either one. Mary always points to Christ, but she does it through the Church. Therefore, we are all called to be Marian people of God.

In the end, I'm not sure why I was granted the miraculous conversion I received, but I firmly vow never to take it for granted. I believe there are no accidents in life, and that everything happens for a reason. For His holy reasons, God the Father gave me new life. And His mother, Our Lady of Medjugorje, helps me to make the most of that life, every day.

Father Donald Calloway, Ohio

"Dear children, today I want to wrap you all in my mantle and lead you all along the way of conversion. Dear children, I beseech you, surrender to the Lord your entire past, all the evil that has accumulated in your hearts. I want each one of you to be happy, but in sin nobody can be happy. Therefore, dear children, pray, and in prayer you shall realize a new way of joy. Joy will manifest in your hearts and thus you shall be joyful witnesses of that which I and my Son want from each one of you. I am blessing you. Thank you for having responded to my call." Message of February 25, 1987

6
Renewing the Church

One of my earliest memories is sitting on my grandmother's lap each night as she prayed the Rosary. When I was too big for her lap, I would sit on the floor by her rocker, listening to the rhythmic sounds of prayer and waiting for the words I loved to hear her say, "This last decade's for you, honey." That sacred evening ritual went on until I was about eight years old. Then, shortly before she died, my grandmother asked me to make her a solemn promise. "Don't ever lose your faith, Mary Sue. Promise me you won't."

That promise was easy to make. After all, how could I possibly lose my faith? We practically *breathed* Catholicity in my family. My mother attended Mass every day and it was part of our daily curriculum in the Catholic school we attended. I grew up with a great devotion to the Blessed Mother, as did my husband, Larry, whom I married in 1957. Neither one of us would have considered marrying someone who wasn't Catholic. Quite simply, our faith was so ingrained in us that we couldn't imagine existing without it.

Back in those days there was a feeling of deep reverence when you entered a Catholic church. I remember that whenever there was trouble in my family, we would go to church to "make a visit." Inside, there was a great silence and we found our strength in the quiet peacefulness of that holy place. Kneeling before the tabernacle, you knew Jesus was there and that He would listen. Everyone in the church knew

He was there; there was never a question that this was the Body and Blood of Christ in the tabernacle and in Holy Communion.

In the mid-1960s, Vatican II changed the Church of my youth and I found my world turned upside down. My wonderful quiet church was gone. Today, I can see what the Church was attempting to do with its reform, but back then it seemed that everything the Church changed made me angry. Despondent, I would go to the earliest Mass possible for the least amount of distraction and sit in the last pew with those who felt alienated but unable to leave. I refused to partake in the sacraments. Perhaps it was the promise that I had made to my grandmother as a child that kept me going to church at all, or the fact that I had nowhere else to go. Larry didn't like the situation either, but he was far more adaptable than I was and his job was his main priority back then, so we didn't really discuss it.

One day, our grade-school-aged children asked us to go to a guitar Mass with them. The idea of guitars in Mass was preposterous to me, but they kept pestering me until finally I said I would go, if they promised never to ask me again. We sat, as usual, in the last pew. Someone asked Larry to bring up the gifts and he agreed. I told him there was no way I was going up there. So Larry and the kids went without me and as I sat there, the loneliness was so oppressive, I couldn't breathe. I remember crying out, "God where are you!" Shaking, I wondered how I could possibly endure this alienation any longer.

That night, a couple we knew stopped by our home. They told us they had just come from a Marriage Encounter weekend and they wanted us to go. They took us to an information night the next week and, within a month, Larry and

I made a Marriage Encounter weekend that changed our lives forever. The weekend took place on the Blessed Mother's birthday, September 8, 1973, and it renewed our love for each other *and* the Church. The Mass on that weekend was incredibly powerful and I was touched in a profound way. It was as if I was hearing those words for the first time, and I fell in love with the liturgy. I believe it was the renewing of my love for Larry that opened my heart and my mind. Since I hadn't been to Confession or Communion in three years, I received both and it felt wonderful to "come home."

Marriage Encounter taught us that in renewing our marriages we are renewing the Church. To me, this was a very powerful concept. The last talk of the weekend asked couples to go forth and serve together. Larry shared with me that our weekend made him realize that God hadn't put him on earth to be president of his company. At that point, we had been married sixteen years, so we made a pledge that we would spend the next sixteen years making up to the Lord for not having served Him. And that's exactly what we did. For the next sixteen years—plus one—we gave many Marriage Encounter weekends, helping hundreds of couples to experience the joy and wonder of their marriage sacrament. We traveled, served in leadership positions, and even edited *Matrimony Magazine,* the official publication for Worldwide Marriage Encounter, for three years without having any previous publishing experience.

Larry and I decided that when our three-year term as editors was over, we were going to retire. We thought we were getting too old to give weekends and besides, our first grandchild was on the way. The two of us were ready to settle into a comfortable life of serving our home parish. About this time, someone gave us money to go to Medjugorje, which was an amazing and generous gift. We went, although a part of me was afraid to go because I thought the Blessed Mother would make a request of us. She didn't. We had a wonderful, spiritual pilgrimage that renewed our love for her. It wasn't that we had ever stopped loving her or praying for her intercession; we used to say Rosaries all the time to get couples to make a weekend. But in Medjugorje, we discovered Our Lady in a new and more meaningful way. We wrote about our experience there in one of the issues of *Matrimony Magazine*.

Father John Birk read our article and called us. He had been to Medjugorje and suggested that we do a retreat there for married couples. So we put an announcement in the magazine and had seventy-five couples and five priests sign up. Our retreat in 1989 took place in an old community house in Bijakovici that was originally used for wedding receptions. One afternoon, a couple came up to us with a question about our talk. We had just given the couples a question to dialogue on, so Larry and I decided to go outside and see if we couldn't clarify that part of the talk to answer the couple's question. As we were walking, we came to the former home of Vicka, one of the visionaries. Larry was just making a suggestion about where to change the talk when I distinctly heard in my right ear, *"I want you to start a Medjugorje magazine in the United States."* I grabbed Larry's arm. Before I could open my mouth, however, Larry stopped dead sentence, looked at me, and said, "Mary Sue, the Blessed Mother wants us to start a Medjugorje magazine in the United States." Incredulous, I told him that I had just heard that same thing in my right ear. To my further amazement, Larry responded, "I know you did." I couldn't believe what he was saying to me, but I also told him I wasn't going to do it. Larry just laughed. I, however, was serious. "I'm not, Larry," I said. "It's been seventeen years, and we have a grandchild now. I just want to spend time with our baby…"

But Larry continued as if I hadn't said anything. He said we couldn't start a magazine alone. Our Lady would have to call two other couples we worked with on *Matrimony Magazine*, Michael and Ann Hatt, who did layouts, and Jerry and Sharon Foote, who owned a publishing company in Florida. Both couples happened to be on retreat with us. "If Our Lady doesn't call them, we can't do it," Larry decided firmly. I reluctantly agreed and told Larry to promise me that he wouldn't say anything to the other couples. They had to hear it from Our Lady directly. And what would the odds of that be? I wondered hopefully. There were three days left on the retreat, and to my relief nothing happened. It looked like we wouldn't have to take on this project after all.

After we had been home for three days, however, Jerry and Sharon phoned. They told us both to get on the line; Jerry had something to tell us. "The Blessed Mother wants us to start a Medjugorje magazine in the United States!" Jerry declared. I instantly dropped to the floor in tears, because I knew there was no getting out of this. When I regained some composure, they asked us if Michael and Ann had said anything about it and we told them they hadn't. We also told them not to mention it. Our Lady had to call this third couple as well or there would be no magazine.

Two months passed and Michael and Ann still did not say anything to us. In fact, they were arguing quite a bit. Both worked full time and they had young children, and Ann was looking forward to the time when they wouldn't have to do *Matrimony Magazine* anymore. One night we were at their home to finish our second-to-last layout for the magazine. In those days, it was all done by hand and we would pray that it wouldn't get lost in the mail. We were praying the Sorrowful Mysteries of the Rosary, when Michael put his head down and started sobbing loudly. Michael is a big man and it really shook me to see him cry such deep, racking sobs. Suddenly, he stopped crying, put his head up and announced, "The Blessed Mother wants us to start a Medjugorje magazine in this country." Ann looked at him in disbelief and then looked at us. "You *know* this, already, don't you?" she demanded. We admitted we did. Ann angrily stormed out of the kitchen, crying and shouting that she wasn't going to do it. After a while, she came back, apologizing. She hadn't, however, changed her mind. She told Mike he could do the magazine, but she was out. I told Ann that we had to do this as couples and we couldn't do it without her. Then I asked her if Our Lady gave her a big sign, would she say yes? Ann quietly agreed.

For the five of us, there was never a doubt that Ann would get her sign; it was simply a matter of when. Each night, Ann would go to bed promptly at ten o'clock. At 10:05 p.m., Michael would call to discuss ideas for the first issue. One night he called and said that once Ann got her sign we needed to interview Martin Sheen because he had just done a documentary about Medjugorje. Larry and I laughed and said, "Oh sure, we'll just knock on his door in California." So Michael, in true Marriage Encounter form, asked us what *our* Impossible Dream was. We answered to have Monsignor Francis Friedl serve as editor with us. Mike retorted that it would be easier to get Martin Sheen than to get Monsignor Friedl.

The next night, Monsignor Friedl, who resides in Dubuque, Iowa, called us. He told us he was in California, and asked us to guess who he had just had dinner with the previous night. "Martin Sheen!" he told us, triumphantly. I thought for sure that Michael had put him up to this, but Monsignor was serious. When I asked him what time he was at dinner, he said eight o'clock, which was ten o'clock our time—the exact hour we were discussing the two of them.

Monsignor Friedl told us that he had talked with Mr. Sheen for two hours. I asked him excitedly if he could write his conversation in interview form for the magazine. He said he could, but he would need to get the actor's approval and Mr. Sheen was leaving at first thing in the morning to make a movie in France. Monsignor phoned his priest friend who had also been at dinner to see if it would be possible to reach the actor in the morning. The priest friend said that Mr. Sheen was stopping by at 6:00 a.m. to pick something up and if the article was ready, he would run it by him. Back in 1989, e-mail was nonexistent and fax machines were hard to come by in the middle of the night. But we were determined. So Monsignor wrote the interview, read it to me over the phone, and I typed it on the computer. Meanwhile, Larry was manning the phones. One of the calls he received was from a man in California. It turned out that the man lived a half-hour away from where Monsignor's priest friend lived *and* he had a fax machine. He agreed to hand-carry the story in the middle of the night and deliver it to the priest. When Martin Sheen arrived, he approved it. Only Our Lady could have worked out the details so perfectly.

The next morning when Ann came down for breakfast, Michael advised her to sit down. He proceeded to tell her the amazing story that had transpired during the night and asked her if this was a big enough sign for her. Ann shook

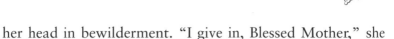

her head in bewilderment. "I give in, Blessed Mother," she finally said, half-laughing and half-crying.

When our last issue of *Matrimony Magazine* was printed, we had a small party for our staff of hard-working volunteers. We announced that we were starting a new magazine about Medjugorje and invited them to join us. Everyone in the room that night decided to stay on. Many of these couples are still with us today, and Monsignor Friedl ended up serving as our spiritual advisor, mentor, and friend.

Our mission for the magazine, since its first issue in 1990, is to spread Our Lady's messages from Medjugorje. Because we are quarterly, we feature the last three monthly messages in every issue. We also report stories of conversions and healings and occasionally interview the visionaries, particularly when they are speaking at conferences in the United States. Over the years, we have organized twelve retreats for married couples in Medjugorje. Our Lady has also asked us to start a Marian Center in Westmont, Illinois, which carries over five thousand traditional Catholic books plus statues, rosaries, and sacramentals, and plays host to annual Marian conferences.

For a long while, Larry and I did a lot of speaking engagements. Our talk was always the same: "How to Live Our Lady's Messages in our Marriages." The Blessed Mother called us as a married couple because we could speak to that. We witnessed women going to Medjugorje and coming back so devoted to God that they would, in a sense, spiritually divorce their husbands. We knew this was not God's plan. Marriage Encounter had taught Larry and me that as a married couple, we are the sign of Jesus' love for His Church. Our Lady would never break the sign of Jesus' love, and we addressed that in our talk. Many women would come up to us afterward, crying, realizing their error and resolving to "return" to their husbands.

It is rewarding for Larry and me to learn how *Medjugorje Magazine* has helped people on their spiritual journeys. Over the years, two calls we received are especially dear to us. Both were from young men considering the priesthood. Each of them said that they went to church to plead with God for a definitive answer to their prayers and when they sat down in the pew, they found a copy of *Medjugorje Magazine*. They picked it up, read it, and took it as their sign to enter the seminary. Both men are priests today. Father Chuck Gallagher, the priest who brought Marriage Encounter to the United States, once asked married couples at a conference to promise him that in their lifetime they would get two men into the seminary. Larry and I made that promise and we consider these to be our two men.

I would say that of all our gifts from Our Lady, our greatest is the conversion that has happened in our own family. For many years, our three children did not understand our enthusiasm for Marriage Encounter or for Medjugorje. They pretty much thought we were fanatics. Larry and I prayed every night for the salvation of our children and our grandchildren, of which there are twelve today. Our Lady heard our pleas and led our children to Medjugorje where they experienced their own individual conversions. They even wrote about their experiences in the magazine, and today our children are as fanatical about their faith as they once accused us of being. Larry and I wish to pass on our Catholic faith to our grandchildren in the same way my grandmother did for me. When our oldest grandchild turned twelve, we asked him if he was old enough to make a lifetime promise. He said he could. We asked him to promise us that he would never leave his Catholic faith, and this has become a private ritual every time a grandchild reaches this age.

The biggest challenge we face with *Medjugorje Magazine* and the Marian Center is that there is no place to store things, and so our home in essence has become a warehouse. While most people our age are downsizing, we had to add a room on to the back of our home. Our former bedroom upstairs has become our office, two more bedrooms are used for storage, and the fourth is a guestroom for visiting friends and family. We sleep in a little room on the main floor. The living room, the foyer, the dining room and even the basement and garage are filled floor to ceiling with magazines, statues, and the like. There is no amount of money in the world that could pay us to give up our home like this. In fact, all of our profits go to Father Jozo's orphans and some orphans in San Salvador. Larry and I have chosen to live this way simply for the messages and for the orphans. That, to us, has been a joy beyond telling.

Father Chuck once told us that Marriage Encounter was the training ground for the work we were going to do in the Church. We have never forgotten those important words; certainly, they have come true for us. He also said we weren't supposed to go out and beat people over the head to come on a Marriage Encounter weekend. People were supposed to see something in our couple-ness, a closeness and a love that they desired in their own marriage. It is the much the same philosophy with Medjugorje. Our Lady tells us not to preach the messages, but to *live* them. Therefore, when people inquire about the happiness they see in Larry and me, we tell them that we are living the messages of Medjugorje.

Marriage Encounter has shown us the powerful graces that flow from the four hands of the marriage sacrament. It helps couples to be better Catholics and renews the world in love. Medjugorje calls *all* people to renew their love for Jesus with messages of hope for our Church and the world today. Living these messages brings people closer to the Lord and closer to His body, the Church. It has brought me back to that same reverence I used to feel in church as a child. Each time I walk into St. James Church in Medjugorje, I experience it. There is no doubt that Jesus is there in that tabernacle. *It's tangible.* While Marriage Encounter helped reawaken in us a tremendous devotion to the Church, Medjugorje renews the devotion to the Heart of the Church—Jesus Christ—truly present in all the tabernacles of the world, and to His mother who leads her children to Him.

Mary Sue and Larry Eck, Illinois

"Dear children, God wants to make you holy. Therefore, through me He is calling you to complete surrender. Let the holy Mass be your life. Understand that the Church is God's palace, the place in which I gather you and want to show you the way to God. Come and pray! Neither look to others nor slander them, but rather let your life be a testimony on the way of holiness. Churches deserve respect and are set apart as holy because God, who became man, dwells in them day and night. Therefore, little children, believe and pray that the Father increases your faith, and then ask for whatever you need. I am with you and I rejoice because of your conversion and I am protecting you with my motherly mantle. Thank you for having responded to my call."

Message of April 25, 1988

7
The Way

My mother, Rosalba, came to America from Italy when she was very young. As a beautiful teenager, she traveled every summer to vacation on the Ionian Coast of Italy, and it was there she met a tall handsome young Italian who would eventually become her husband and my father. Although my mother's parents disagreed with the engagement, my mother married him against their wishes. The young couple eventually relocated to the United States and settled in the north end of Boston, known as Little Italy, where their marriage was an unhappy one. My father was a jealous and controlling man who was impossible to live with. He abused my mother physically and emotionally, and it is truly a miracle that she is still alive today to tell about it.

I am thoroughly convinced that the only reason my mother survived her torment is that she sought consolation by going to Mass and various healing services. She would pray constantly for a change in her situation and for God's protection. When my mother found out that she was pregnant a third time (with me), her doctor counseled her to seek an abortion because of the problems at home. My mother, however, knew this was out of the question. She had learned the hard way that abortion is murder, and if God was sending her a child now, it would simply have to be.

The night I was born, my mother nearly died. The doctor had given her the wrong anesthetic and it caused major complications. She describes the moment as a very frightening experience in which she felt as though she were fading away until she finally found herself in a black, empty place. "I prayed an Our Father and suddenly the frightful sight turned into Our Lord Jesus," my mother told me later. That's when she realized that Jesus had come to take her place in suffering. Next she felt as if she were falling from the universe through white and pink clouds, landing eventually on her hospital bed. When my mother regained consciousness, she asked the hospital staff what had happened. They told her there had been an emergency, causing great danger to both her and her child. The medical team thought they were going to lose her, but it is quite obvious that God had other plans.

After nine long years of torment, my mother finally had the courage to divorce my father and seek an annulment, which she was successful in obtaining. From that point on, she decided to dedicate her life solely to God and her children, because it was God who had saved her. Her life was not easy, considering that my father never paid child support, and my mother often had to work several jobs just to keep the household going. However, she never despaired through these trials because she knew that with God, all things were possible. Fortunately, my mother received constant support from her wonderful parents, who had also relocated to the United States from Italy. My siblings and I considered them second parents and we were delighted to purchase a home together in Massachusetts.

As part of my mother's promise to God, she began taking her children to Sunday Mass as well as healing services and Medjugorje conferences. My mother had never been there, but she became a firm believer in the apparitions after seeing a video about it. Being a child at the time, I didn't understand much about Medjugorje, but for some reason I always accepted the fact that the Blessed Mother was appearing there. I will never forget an experience I had at one particular conference that my family and I had attended in Worcester, Massachusetts. My mother brought me up to meet Ivan Dragicevic, the visionary, who looked me square in the eye and said to my mother, "Be strict with her." Ivan knew what he was talking about. Although my mother was a very strict parent, especially with me, I was still a spoiled and rebellious child, often referred to as the "little terror" of the three. From middle school to high school, my behavior continued on much the same path. To make matters worse, my beloved grandmother "Nonna Nina" was diagnosed with leukemia, and I spent much of my time comforting her and taking care of her.

Nonna Nina had always had a strong faith in God, but during her battle with cancer she began to pray in earnest, growing less afraid and more willing to accept God's will. Two nights before she died, my grandmother called out my mother's name and asked her to come into her bedroom. She told my mother that she had had the same dream two nights in a row in which she was in Medjugorje and Jesus was there. He was walking along the road with His disciples and He came to her and said, "Nina, I will heal you." However, at the end of the dream she said she saw four emergency medical technicians (EMTs) enter her room and take her out on a stretcher. My mother was very touched by this dream. She promised Nonna Nina that she would have a replica of the Medjugorje cross built on some land we owned in Italy, so that people could see it and reflect on the love God has for us by dying on the cross in order that we may live forever with Him.

That night, my grandmother died. It was a night I will never forget, standing there feeling afraid and watching her being rolled away on a stretcher by four EMTs. I grieved as though I had lost my own mother. As promised, my mother arranged to have a cross built on a mountaintop overlooking the Ionian Coast of southern Italy, bringing inspiration and hope to travelers in that region. Two years later, my wonderful grandfather passed away too, saying that he missed his wife and wanted to be with her in heaven. It was a very trying time in my life and I started acting out in self-destructive ways. Fortunately, my mother never gave up on me. She saw all of this as a test to prove our faith and trust in God. She knew God loved us and that somehow things would work out.

In college, I changed majors several times, dabbling in theater and film before graduating with a degree in psychology with a pre-med track. My plan was to be a doctor. By the time I graduated, I was still searching spiritually. One night my mother took me to hear a Catholic author by the name of Matthew Kelly, a passionate young man who speaks to a generation of youth searching for meaning in life deeper than the pursuit of pleasure and possessions. His main point is that who we are or who we become is infinitely more important than what we do or what we have. I was truly impressed with Matthew's message and his words challenged me to think about what I was doing with my own life.

I also had opportunities to hear Ivan from Medjugorje speak again, and each time I did I felt a renewed interest in following Our Lady's requests to pray. I realized I had to make a choice with my life, because I could no longer serve two masters as scripture says. I was either going to follow God, the right way, or follow the rest of the world, the wrong way. I began to pray earnestly and ask God to lead me where He wanted me to be, and that's exactly what He did.

It was at a healing service at the Fatima Shrine in Holliston, Massachusetts, on a summer night in 2003 when I experienced an important turning point in my life. A woman praying over me looked at me with these piercing blue eyes and said, "Our Lord wants you to visit Him more often; go and visit." I was confused and surprised to hear these words, because I felt that attending Sunday Mass was spending ample time with God. At the same time, however, an overpowering sensation had taken hold of me. Driving home that night, I pondered the woman's words. Was it true, did Jesus really want me to visit Him?

That night, I had a dream. It felt so real, I'm not sure it wasn't more of a vision. In it, I encountered the Blessed Mother in the image of Our Lady of Guadaloupe, although I am not sure why she appeared to me in that way as I did not have a devotion to this image. She placed her hand on my left shoulder and all I can remember is that it was cool to the touch. My reaction was a mixture of joy and fear and I could only think to shout for my mother who was sleeping upstairs; however, she was unable to hear me. I asked the Virgin, "Why aren't you allowing my mother to hear me?" and she replied, *"Monica, first say your prayers and only then will your mother hear you."* She handed me a piece of white paper with three prayers on it and I began saying the prayers immediately, but when I woke up I couldn't remember what they were. It also became clear to me in time that what Our Lady meant about not being heard until I started praying was not a reference to my earthly mother, but to my spiritual mother in heaven.

Soon after, I began to visit the tabernacle regularly where I could be with Jesus in the Blessed Sacrament and pray with the heart. Through this intimate experience with God, I gained clarity in my life. I realized that my passion was not for the field of medicine, but for the arts, specifically music. Through prayer, I became inspired to write songs and become a Christian artist. I soon understood that this was more than a career choice—it was my mission. I prayed that God would use me as His instrument through the gift of music to bring about a change within the hearts of my listeners.

God has taken me up on my prayer and has assisted me not only in writing my own music, but learning how to mix, edit, and record it. The fruits of this is a compact disc (CD) entitled "The Way." The music, a mix of electronic/rock/pop sounds, is something totally new to the Catholic music scene. The intent of my music is to spread truth to the young generation that is in most need. There are so many voices today distorting truth in every aspect of our culture. The media is doing a great disservice by bombarding us with all types of offenses and trying to undermine our intellect and desensitize us. Having once been one of those impoverished youths, hypnotized by today's persuasive culture, I feel called through my gift of music to make a change. My hope is that when people listen to my music they can move beyond the beat and enter into the world of words—words of consolation, comfort, and encouragement.

Because of my mother's prayers, unceasing devotion, and search for the truth, I was led to the Blessed Mother, who in turn led me to Our Lord. I now realize it is only with God that we can survive the many trials and tribulations we face in this world. Without Him, I would not have peace or joy, nor would my musical success be possible. It amazes me today that I was so indifferent to God in my younger life. It was not as if I ever disbelieved in His existence, because I had many spiritual experiences in my childhood to remind me. But somehow, I allowed myself to forget to include God in my life, and as a result I lost my direction. I'm so grateful that through prayer, He has helped me find the way—the only way.

Monica Ursino, Massachusetts

"Dear children, today I call you to decide for God during these days. You, young people, put God at the first place in your life; thus you will have with Him a way that is sure. I invite you to pray for my intentions of peace."
Message of August 2, 1992

8
Works of Mercy

The practice of doing works of mercy—offering compassion and assistance to those in need—was something I was taught early in life through the generous hospitality of my Maronite Catholic parents. My mother was from Lebanon, and had been visiting the United States in 1952 when she met my father, a first-generation Lebanese. He liked her immediately and invited her to Buffalo, New York, to meet his family. When she didn't show up on the appointed date, my father and his father drove from Buffalo to Olean, New York, and knocked on her door to see what had happened. The young Lebanese woman looked my father straight in the eye and said, "I told the Blessed Mother that if you were the one, you would come back for me." And so they were married two weeks later and settled on the west side of Buffalo.

My father was an apprentice for a carpet installer and a bread deliverer for a local baker. My mother was a great cook and butcher, as her father and grandfather had been before her. Together, my parents opened a bakery on Grant Street, where my father spent a part of his day helping to bake and deliver bread. In addition to their work at the bakery, it was a common occurrence for our family to host Lebanese immigrants coming to America to start a new life. It was perfectly normal for me to give up my bedroom on a regular basis and sleep on the couch in the living room. Although our immediate family was small, it never seemed that way because my mother cooked for twenty people every day and our table was always set.

Our Lebanese guests were fleeing from the Turkish war and they often had to leave family behind. Therefore, when one of these immigrants passed away in their new country, the surviving spouse was truly alone. My father would go to church on Sunday and stay for three Masses so he could pick up all the widowers and bring them home, where my mother would cook a big meal. He also took care of the widows and orphans by checking on them regularly. I didn't know at the time that what my parents were doing was called works of mercy; I just knew that it helped people and it was what God would want us to do.

By high school, I decided I wanted to be a sister with the Niagara Franciscans, but I was told to get a college education and work a few years first. This was a great disappointment for me. I didn't want to wait; I wanted to begin helping others immediately. I enrolled in college but it made me miserable, so I dropped out and took a job at a bank. Eventually they put me to work in collections, which I did well because I learned to listen to people who were having financial difficulties and help them get back on their feet.

My relationship with God was strong because of the great love I experienced from my earthly father, but my "rejection" by the Franciscan sisters made me upset with Him. When my local parish cancelled a Mass in order to have an anti-war demonstration on its premises, I got angry with the priests as well and stopped going to Sunday Mass. I did, however, visit church almost daily to talk with Jesus in the Blessed Sacrament, a habit I had begun in grammar school.

In 1981, a donut shop that my cousin owned was up for sale. I had always wanted to open a restaurant since I was a child, and with my parents' help, I purchased it, leaving my job at the bank. For the first three years, I ran it as a New York deli and established a solid customer base. When the local university closed, however, it hurt my business and I thought I might have to shut down. A group of men who frequented the shop encouraged me not to quit because they said I was doing a good thing for the community. They told me that if I stayed open they would help me build a new restaurant. The end result was an establishment called "Amy's Place."

I worked hard, seven days a week, polishing my cooking skills and getting to know the locals. My restaurant turned out to be more than a place to come for a good meal. God was beginning to guide me during this time and show me that my real business was helping people. Whatever people needed—food, a little financial help, prayers, or advice— they could come to Amy's Place. Word got out and the restaurant was always busy. We weren't making a fortune, but we were making a difference.

In 1989, my cousin Anna went to Medjugorje, a place I had never heard of before. When she came back I could tell she was deeply affected. When I asked her what God was saying through the messages, she told me, "God is upset with His people because they have left the churches, synagogues, and temples. They are all empty. God wants us to return to Him." This news hit me hard because I wasn't going to Sunday Mass myself. In fact, the restaurant kept me so busy, I wasn't even stopping into church like I used to. I was one of those people upsetting God. This prompted me to return to church and begin praying the Rosary.

By Christmas that year, I experienced what I call a "St. Paul" conversion. My uncle was visiting from Lebanon and he was "reading the cups," an old Lebanese tradition. Studying the Turkish coffee grinds, he said to me very seriously, "The Blessed Mother loves you very much. Your life will change, but you must go to the church closest to you. Do you know where that is?" I told him yes, there was one across the street from the restaurant. "She wants you to go," said my uncle. "She's waiting for you." I went home, mulling this over. My girlfriend, who was staying with our family at the time, handed me a newspaper that someone had left for me. The cover headline read, "Our Lady Queen of Peace Visits Medjugorje." I began to weep and could not stop. In the ensuing days, I cried in my sleep; I cried when I was awake; I cried when I was working. People thought I was having a nervous breakdown. The more I read that paper, the more I cried. One of the articles talked about the steps of conversion that the Blessed Mother was asking of her children: daily Mass, weekly fasting, monthly Confession, praying the Rosary, and reading scripture. I wanted to do it all at once. I went out and bought myself a Bible, books on the saints, and everything I could find about Medjugorje.

The more I read, the more on fire I became for the Lord. New Year's Eve that year fell on a Sunday. I was working in the restaurant when a TV program came on called *The Lasting Sign,* a documentary about Medjugorje with Martin Sheen. For one solid hour, the whole restaurant seemed to stop. No one came in or out and no one asked for anything during their meal. I watched the show and was blown away, crying through the entire program. Immediately after, I went to the church across the street and knelt before the statue of the Blessed Mother. In prayer, I consecrated my life to her in order to do her Son's work. While I was praying, gazing upon the Blessed Mother, I had a vision in my mind's eye. It was of a little girl, about seven years old, who had just finished watching the movie *Song of Bernadette* about the visionary of Lourdes. It took me a moment to recognize that the little girl was me. I watched as she ran to her mother's bedroom, flopped on the bed, and cried, "Oh Blessed Mother, if only you would appear while I am alive, I would give you my life." At that moment, kneeling before the statue of the Blessed Mother, I realized that the childhood promise I had made—but had long forgotten—was being fulfilled today. From that day on, my entire life changed.

I made a trip to Medjugorje in May of 1990, where I consecrated myself formally. The months leading up to my pilgrimage were spent in prayerful preparation. I gave up smoking as a gift to the Lord and also went to Confession after having been away from the sacrament for eighteen years. It was an unforgettable event, as though someone had lifted a two-hundred-pound boulder from my shoulders. Later, one of my customers even commented that I was glowing. I'm sure I was. God had just given me the grace to recognize the sins I had committed for eighteen long years, and then He forgave them all in an instant! What amazing mercy, that allows us to start all over again.

I liken my conversion to St. Paul's for several reasons. Like St. Paul, I was shown my wretchedness and still received forgiveness. The great saint was blinded for seven days; I cried for seven days. He got to visit heaven; I got to visit Medjugorje, which is like heaven on earth. Being in that holy place and seeing what I saw, feeling what I felt, and learning what I learned will last me a lifetime.

For the next two years, God really started working on my heart, healing me, teaching me, and preparing me. I went to every healing Mass and talk I could and got baptized in the

Holy Spirit. I started a Medjugorje prayer group called "Mary's People" and spent long hours in adoration. We traveled to various parishes, showed *The Lasting Sign,* spoke about the apparitions, and I shared my conversion story. In Medjugorje, the Blessed Mother asks her children to read Matthew 6:24 every week. It's the reading about not being able to serve two masters—God *and* money—and about trusting the Lord with our life and future. I meditated on this reading every day for a year until it became a part of my essence.

It was during this time that my father passed away. I loved my father dearly, and would go as far as saying that he was my greatest attachment on earth. His death was difficult to accept, but my acceptance of it was necessary in order to go where the Lord was leading me. It was the proper order. God also used this time to teach me the skills of evangelization. He used my restaurant as a training ground and taught me how not to be afraid of the world. I had some people tell me that when they walked by my restaurant, they heard a voice in their ear say to them, "*Go in. She'll feed you.*" Often, I discovered that people needed to be fed spiritually as well. They needed someone to pray for them. We freely gave away medals, holy cards, and rosaries that we kept in our cash registers. The Lord also taught me to put people's intentions in my heart and offer up my day for them.

All kinds of people would come to Amy's Place: Muslims, Jews, Christians, atheists, and others. God showed me how to love them all with truth and kindness. To me, they were all children of God. One of the things I felt compelled to bring back from Medjugorje to display in the restaurant was a picture of the Blessed Mother in which she had no face. Often, in conversing with customers, I would talk about God, but when someone came in and commented specifically about the picture, I understood this to mean that I should direct my conversation toward the Blessed Mother. I would explain, for example, that the Virgin Mary is the mother of all of us, so we can put our face where hers ought to be, and that's what she looks like.

In 1991, my prayer group began brainstorming ideas to celebrate the upcoming seventy-fifth anniversary of the apparitions of Fatima. We coordinated events with various Marian groups throughout the city and, through these endeavors, I met Auxiliary Bishop Edward M. Grosz of Buffalo on the Feast of the Immaculate Conception. He called me shortly afterward and invited me to accompany him to Fatima. How could I say no? Not long after I placed my deposit, a water main broke and our restaurant was flooded. What should have been a disaster ended up being a blessing, because many of my customers came together to help repair and remodel the restaurant, making it even better than before, which would be providential to God's plans.

During my trip to Fatima I met Norm Paolini, Jr., a family man and talented musician who shared my passion for doing works of mercy, particularly for God's lost and forgotten children. I discovered on my trip that Fatima, like Medjugorje, is a very special place. In Medjugorje, I discovered that Jesus really loved me. In Fatima, I fell in love with Him, in a spiritually deep and mature way. I felt a true freedom from worldly things and all I cared about was being with Jesus. After our pilgrimage, Bishop Grosz asked Norm and me to accompany him to Fatima a second time with a group of fifteen young people. We accepted. In the months between these two pilgrimages, Norm and I began to collaborate in our efforts to serve the people of the east side of

Buffalo, working together through an organization he established called "Madonna of the Street."

During our second trip to Fatima, we learned that St. Luke's Roman Catholic Church in Buffalo had closed and the building was up for sale. It was a beautiful old church with the only image of the Divine Mercy in the entire city. Norm and I asked the kids on the pilgrimage to pray with us about the future of that building. While we were praying, I discerned that the Blessed Mother wanted me to purchase it because she desired to make it her center for Divine Mercy. I reported my discernment to the Auxiliary Bishop. Apparently, there were other parties interested in purchasing the property. I met with Bishop Edward D. Head of the Diocese of Buffalo and told him that we proposed to open a mission house at St. Luke's that would rely on donations and not diocesan funding. I sold my newly remodeled restaurant and gave up everything I had, but it was not enough to purchase St. Luke's. Still, I was confident that if Jesus wanted the building, it would happen. Norm and I began praying novenas for the balance of the money required and through this we were inspired to approach Eileen Nanula, a woman Norm knew from a charismatic prayer group who was in her own discernment process about how to serve the Lord. The St. Luke's building seemed a perfect fit, and she generously donated the needed balance. On August 1, 1994, Norm and I opened the doors of St. Luke's Mission of Mercy to assist the people on the East side of Buffalo.

When we bought St. Luke's, it was established that we could not have Mass in the church without permission from the bishop because we were not intended to be a parish. We could, however, have Mass in the chapel on any day except Sunday. We also had permission to house the Blessed

Sacrament in the tabernacle, which I stipulated in the contract because I could not embark on this endeavor without the Lord. The church was in great shape, with the altars and pews still intact. Father Dennis Mancuso, a holy priest and dear friend, taught us how to care for our church. He helped us decorate it so that it was liturgically correct, using many donated items from the Felician Sisters, who were closing down some of their convents. Father Dennis celebrated our first Mass in the chapel and served as our first unofficial pastor at the mission. Since the earliest days, we have included Jesus in the Eucharist and the guidance of a priest in every decision and at every stage of development at St. Luke's, and I believe this has been the key to the mission's success.

People who have no place to turn for food, shelter, guidance, counsel, and love come through our doors every day, and we are made better because of them. Starting with our first homeless guest, each resident has taught us something that we believe the Lord wishes us to learn. The experience of reaching out to God's children is a joyful one, but not without its challenges. Oftentimes there is violence and unpredictable behavior owing to the deep wounds that our residents bear. Over the course of time, something interesting began to happen. The people we were assisting knew that Norm and I and our growing staff of missionaries were devout Catholics. We would talk to them about Jesus and invite them to worship with us at the local parish we attended. Some of the residents expressed an interest in joining the Church. This led to several of the missionaries becoming RCIA and CCD catechists, and we sponsored a growing number of people into the faith. When transporting these converts to church became unwieldy, I approached the bishop about our unique problem and we were given per-

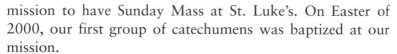

mission to have Sunday Mass at St. Luke's. On Easter of 2000, our first group of catechumens was baptized at our mission.

Each year, more and more ministries are spawned from St. Luke's. God is so good and gracious to us. We have a wonderful group of people known as the FOSLs, or "Friends of St. Luke's," who support our mission with their time and talent. We have opened a Don Bosco House for high school–aged boys who can no longer live at home and a Good Shepherd Residence for men recovering from alcohol and other addictions. A number of our missionaries have formed the *Voices of Mercy,* which provides beautiful original music for liturgies, concerts, retreats, and other functions we are invited to attend.

Today there are over one hundred lay people in our extended missionary community. We also have a full-time priest on board with us, Jesuit Father Jack Maramore, whom God most assuredly sent our way. In addition to Norm and me, there are fifteen missionaries who live at St. Luke's, and we are currently in the process of applying for recognition as a lay community. We have written a rule for the bishop and we wear St. Benedict crucifixes around our necks, which has become a highly recognized symbol of St. Luke's Mission of Mercy.

There are clear signs that the inner city of Buffalo is being rejuvenated, including the recent construction of a new Catholic church on this side of town. Yet, there is much more to do. While we have acquired a number of houses in the neighborhood through donation, we are always filled to capacity. Future plans include a bed-and-breakfast for the homeless and a group home for the mentally ill. This will cost millions, but we trust that Jesus will move the hearts of the faithful to help us raise the money as He has done throughout our ten-year history.

Changes have certainly come to and been brought about by St. Luke's over the years, but one thing remains the same, and that is our mission. We are committed to God's call to evangelize, preaching with our lives the Good News of Jesus Christ. Our work and our very being centers on Jesus present in the Eucharist and our mission is to bring the love and mercy of God to those who feel abandoned by Him. Together, we work toward a fullness of life for people of all ages, cultures, social status, and faiths using the tools of unconditional acceptance, peaceful understanding, and loving forgiveness. Our philosophy is that Jesus stills suffers and thirsts in those in need. Therefore, in serving them, we are serving Him.

Amy Betros, New York

"Dear children, today I invite you to do works of mercy with love and out of love for me and for your and my brothers and sisters. All that you do for others, do it with great joy and humility towards God. I am with you, and day after day I offer your sacrifices and prayers to God for the salvation of the world. Thank you for having responded to my call!"
Message of November 25, 1990

9
The True Presence

My parish, St. Bernadette's Roman Catholic Church in Orchard Park, New York, recently celebrated seven years of perpetual adoration of the Blessed Sacrament. This devotion has brought numerous blessings to our parish, both for the pastor and the parishioners. In Pope John Paul II's encyclical *Ecclesia de Eucharistia* (The Church of the Eucharist), the Holy Father states that it is the responsibility of every pastor to encourage adoration. To further his point, he instituted a Year of the Eucharist to elevate our understanding and appreciation of the Blessed Sacrament. Over the past several years, St. Bernadette's has witnessed firsthand the many graces and miracles that are attributed to eucharistic adoration. How it came to our parish—and how I became one of the coordinators—is somewhat of a miracle in itself.

I was baptized in the Catholic Church, a cradle Catholic, but growing up I had little knowledge of my faith. I remember that my mother had a strong devotion to the Blessed Virgin Mary and I can still picture her leading the Rosary in front of her statue of Our Lady of Fatima during the months of May and October. My budding faith, however, would be challenged by a series of childhood traumas. My father was killed in a plant explosion when I was five and I was too young to draw on my faith for comfort and understanding. Not long after the loss of my father, my mother remarried into an unhealthy relationship. My stepfather was an alcoholic who brought physical and sexual abuse into the family, resulting in dark and painful years for all of us. One evening, trying to find something good in being locked in our bedroom, my sister and I looked in the dictionary and realized that our last name, Emanuele, meant "God with Us." This gave us great comfort and we knew that somehow we would endure our pain because God would look out for us.

In my late teens, a typical time for questioning and searching, changes in the Church introduced by Vatican II added more confusion to my spirituality. It was further weakened when my stepfather left home, leaving my mother, who had no employable skills, to raise six children. I blamed God for all of our hardships and told my mother that I would not attend Sunday Mass anymore. In 1969, I was married and overjoyed to become pregnant with our first child, but my joy turned to despair when I began to experience bleeding in the first trimester. My doctor called it a "threatened abortion" and in my case, my body's threats were real: I lost my first child. It was a devastating time for me, causing me a great deal of suffering in my marriage and in my personal life. I almost lost our next baby, Thomas, through another threatened abortion, but by the grace of God I was able to make it through the entire nine months. Eighteen months later we had a beautiful healthy little girl, Alanna, with no difficulty at all.

Because of the trauma I experienced in my childhood, I wanted peace and stability for my children. Deep down, I knew that the only answer was to refocus my life on God and lead my children in His ways, but the truth was I was still having a difficult time trusting Him. I wanted to do things my way. Having experienced the loss of a child, I was extremely upset to discover that my sister had given her son Joey up to foster care so that she could run off with a man.

My mother and I knew nothing about her decision or we would have cared for her little boy. When we discovered the news, my mother tried everything possible to find the child, but in those days this was a difficult task at best. In desperation, I began to pray the one prayer that was still familiar to me: the Rosary. Every night as I prayed those beautiful mysteries and pleaded for help in finding little Joey, I could feel the Blessed Mother close to me. It was such a warm and peaceful feeling. I promised Our Lady that I would remain faithful to her if she would help us to find my nephew. Remarkably, my mother was able to find where the child was a short time later and was even able to visit him, which was unheard of at that time. I was so convinced that my prayers had been answered and that I had experienced a miracle, I kept my promise to Our Lady. I returned to the Church and continued praying the Rosary.

In 1985, I learned that the Virgin Mary was appearing in Medjugorje to six children. I read as much as I could about the apparitions and knew in my heart that some day I would travel there. A few years later, in 1990, I joined a Medjugorje prayer group that was started on September 8, the Blessed Mother's birthday. The following April, our pastor, Monsignor Richard Nugent, decided to lead a pilgrimage to Medjugorje. I wanted to go very badly, but I did not have the money to pay for such a trip, or so I thought. As fate would have it, I received an insurance settlement from a car accident that my husband and I were involved in some time before. It was the exact amount needed to send my daughter, Alanna, and me on the pilgrimage. While it was not the most convenient time for her, as she was in her first year of college and had exams to study for, Alanna was willing to go. Neither of us had ever traveled abroad before, so there was a certain excitement about the whole adventure. We had heard many amazing stories about Medjugorje, but both of us were in agreement that we would not look for any signs; we just wanted to be where Our Lady was.

On the first day of our pilgrimage, our group was scheduled to meet at St. James to climb Apparition Hill to be present for an apparition. Alanna, ever the strong-willed and independent young lady, convinced me that we could find Apparition Hill on our own. As we followed the crowds and reached the designated spot marked by crosses, I happened to look over to the larger mountain, Mount Krizevac, across the valley. To my utter amazement, I saw a vision of Our Lady in which she appeared in a rainbow of colors. She was standing in front of the cross at the top of the mountain, her hands folded as she prayed over the valley in the direction of St. James Church. A group of pilgrims from Ireland seated on a nearby rock was also able to see this vision. To Alanna's great disappointment, she could not see what we were looking at so intently in the distance. The next day, however, Alanna would get her turn. We had gone to St. James for Mass, but could not get inside the building due to the large crowds. Therefore, we had to stand outside with many others, listening to the Rosary being broadcast on outdoor speakers. During the time of the apparition, we noticed that the birds that had been so busy chirping and hopping around on the choir loft windows became silent and perfectly still for several minutes. As Alanna gazed up at the choir loft window, she said softly that she could see intermittent flashes of light during the time of the apparition. It gave her a feeling of tremendous peace.

Medjugorje was the first place my daughter had found peace in a long while. She, like her mother, had endured her share of trauma growing up. As a young teenager, Alanna had to deal with the deaths of some children she used to babysit for, who perished in a house fire. She loved these children and would often tell them stories about Our Lady appearing in Medjugorje, although they were Presbyterian. It was discovered that the stepfather was responsible for the fire, and Alanna had to testify at the trial twice before the age of sixteen to help put him behind bars for life. She never quite got over this ordeal and the loss of those little children.

The two of us experienced another moment of tremendous peace on Thursday night of our pilgrimage in Medjugorje. After Rosary, Mass, and prayers for the sick, we remained inside St. James and watched as the entire village seemed to file in to join the pilgrims. There were fathers, mothers, sons, daughters, grandparents; it seemed as if no one was left at home. Soon St. James was packed to capacity with absolutely no standing room left inside. There was an excitement and an anticipation building among the people, and at first we weren't sure why. Then we spotted what everyone was looking at: the priests were processing around the church and blessing the people with a vessel that one of them held regally in the air. As the priest passed by us with his treasure, my daughter and I were suddenly overcome with awe and tears of joy. For the first time in my life I understood that the Eucharist, which was what the priest was presenting to us, is really and truly Jesus Christ. He was here that night, among us! The whole atmosphere in the church was so Spirit-filled that I felt myself lifted to a new and deeper level of love for my Savior. It was a defining moment for me and I realized that I would never be the same again.

When I returned home from Medjugorje, I became an evangelist for Jesus' true presence in the Blessed Sacrament.

I read and meditated on the Gospel of John 6:51, "If anyone eat of this bread, he will live forever; and the bread that I will give is my flesh for the life of the world." The words illuminated my soul. Imagine, Jesus Christ, truly present— Body, Blood, Soul and Divinity—for me...for all of us! How could I have been so lost in myself that I did not recognize His true presence? I had so much to be thankful for. Yes, I had had my share of crosses in life, but I had received so many more blessings. I realized that through all of the crosses, Jesus had been there to help me carry them.

Not long after my pilgrimage, one of the ladies in our prayer group asked me if I would be willing to do a Holy Hour for a First Friday devotion in our parish. At first I wasn't sure what she meant by a "Holy Hour." Then the Holy Spirit helped me to understand that this is exactly what I had experienced in the tiny village of Medjugorje. On that awesome Thursday night at St. James, all of us were adoring Jesus present in the Holy Eucharist. The priest had processed with the consecrated host in that beautiful vessel (which I later learned was called the monstrance) and as he traveled throughout the church I was totally enrapt. And now I had the opportunity to be in the sacred presence of Jesus for an hour each month in my own parish. I eagerly agreed.

When I told Monsignor Nugent about my spiritual awakening in Medjugorje, he advised me not to tell anyone that I hadn't realized that Jesus was present in the Blessed Sacrament. "Every Catholic knows that, Joanne," he said. I replied, "Father, if I, a practicing Catholic, didn't recognize and believe in Jesus' true presence, I'm sure there are many others who don't understand this, either." Then I read a survey that was administered to practicing Catholics, which reported that a shocking 68 percent of them did not believe that Jesus was truly present in the Eucharist. Wow, I thought to myself. The problem was worse than I thought! I recalled how St. James was filled with the local farmers and their families praying together in total submission. What was wrong with us in America? Were we too educated and sophisticated to pray?

When I learned that a local parish had perpetual adoration, I approached Monsignor Nugent about doing the same thing at St. Bernadette's. Fortunately, our pastor had the wisdom to recognize that our parish was not quite ready for that. He did, however, allow our prayer group to initiate a twenty-four-hour period of adoration on First Fridays. On October 2, 1992, the Feast of the Guardian Angels, we began this practice, inviting families and school children to make a Holy Hour and to pray for family life, vocations, and peace.

Our prayer group was encouraged by the turnout and we approached Monsignor Nugent again about perpetual adoration, not realizing the intense undertaking it would require. Again, our pastor used good judgment. He wanted to carefully nourish the parish's growing interest in the Blessed Sacrament and told us if we could get enough people to sign up for hourly adoration, from nine o'clock in the morning to nine o'clock in the evening, Monday through Friday, he would eventually consider perpetual adoration. I had planned a second trip to Medjugorje around this time, and I went seeking the confidence to lead such an endeavor in my parish. During my trip, the visionary Vicka prayed over me for a long time. Although I did not understand her words, I felt fortified by her prayers for me and I returned home from that trip a daily communicant.

One morning, when I was receiving the Eucharist in my hand, I noticed to my great astonishment rays of light coming out from it. I could barely get back to my seat, I was so overcome, and I have not received Communion in the hand since. This private miracle seemed to be a confirmation that Jesus was asking me to lead the parish toward daily adoration, but at first I was so afraid that I started going to Mass at other parishes to avoid this responsibility. How could I be the one to lead such an endeavor? I had barely made it through religious education. The Lord was patient with me and in His infinite wisdom, He inspired enough people to sign up for the entire week without any conflicts. Because of the ease of filling the hours, we knew in our hearts that God wanted this. On the Feast of the Holy Rosary, October 7, 1994, we began daily adoration with a concert by the wonderful Irish tenor and Medjugorje convert, David Parkes. Our Lady further blessed our efforts when the visionary Ivan Dragicevic came to St. Bernadette's on October 10 and had his daily apparition with over one thousand people in attendance.

In 1997, Monsignor Nugent felt we were ready to move to perpetual adoration. He invited the Missionaries of the Blessed Sacrament to speak at all Masses on the weekend of September 14, the Triumph of the Cross, to inspire our parishioners. At last, five years after our original request, perpetual adoration was a reality. We now have families—fathers, mothers, sons, and daughters—honoring Our Lord twenty-four hours a day, seven days a week. Once again, as if to confirm and approve our efforts, Our Lady brought Ivan back to St. Bernadette's on October 9 for another apparition and Monsignor had plaques made to honor the Blessed Mother's presence.

Perpetual adoration at St. Bernadette's has yielded tremendous fruits in our parish. With the increased understanding of Jesus' true presence in the Blessed Sacrament, there has been an increase in Mass attendance and in people returning to the faith. We are seeing young fathers praying for their families; teenagers signing up for hours of adoration; children released from drug abuse; marriages saved from divorce; and an increase in prayer groups and priestly vocations. A number of ministries have started at St. Bernadette's since we began perpetual adoration. We have a Family Ministry that has developed a library of Catholic books and videos for parish use, a Youth Ministry that participates in activities like World Youth Day, a Pro-Life Ministry that invites priests in our diocese to preach on life, a St. Joseph's Table to benefit the poor, a Divine Mercy Ministry to visit the dying, and a new Catholic apologetics group. We even have a music ministry called "Lazarus Awakening" that travels to other parishes to provide music for Mass and a Holy Hour with the Blessed Sacrament.

In addition to the blessings we have seen on a parish level, I have experienced my own personal consolations and graces from adoration. Perhaps most notable is the way the Lord listens to my prayers for my daughter, Alanna. A couple of years after our initial pilgrimage to Medjugorje, Alanna's college roommate had been raped and beaten almost to the point of death and my daughter was one of the girls who found her. This crime, and the one that caused the death of the children she babysat for, was too much for Alanna. She suffered great emotional pain because of it, losing her faith in mankind, in her religion, and, for a time, in God. For many years, she searched earnestly for peace and meaning to life in places other than her Catholic faith. She explored Hinduism, Buddhism, the New Age movement, and yoga. For a while some of these things delivered a degree of peace, but none of it seemed to be lasting or complete. I prayed before the Blessed Sacrament that Our Lady would cover Alanna with her mantle as she continued in her spiritual journey.

In 2002, I felt a need to return to Medjugorje to thank the Blessed Mother for helping me initiate perpetual adoration at St. Bernadette's. It was Alanna's thirtieth birthday and I was delighted when she accepted my invitation to join me on the pilgrimage. For a number of years, Alanna had been coordinating yoga and surf retreats in Costa Rica. Because the ocean water was polluted and she had not been changing her contact lenses regularly, vision-impairing ulcerations developed in her eyes. Her doctor told Alanna she had a 50 percent chance of going blind and did not think she should travel out of the country. Still, I persuaded her to come with me. We were going to be staying with Ivan's family in Medjugorje, where we would be privileged to be in attendance for an apparition. Surely the Blessed Mother could help my daughter.

By the time we made all of our plane connections and arrived in Medjugorje, Alanna could not see at all. She was miserable and angry that I had dragged her halfway around the world, especially because she had begun to doubt the visionaries were still witnessing Our Lady's appearances. As soon as we got to Ivan's house, he said it was time to prepare for the apparition. He knelt and the rest of us followed suit and joined him in praying the Rosary. When Ivan's voice stopped abruptly, indicating the apparition was taking place, I kept feeling Alanna elbowing me in the ribs. "Look!" she whispered under her breath. "I see two angels." I did not see anything. After the apparition, Ivan told the people gathered that Our Lady had appeared dressed in white and that two angels had preceded her. I was amazed at this announcement and even more astonished to discover that Alanna's sight was immediately and completely restored. Equally important, her acceptance of the apparitions in Medjugorje was restored as well.

Today, Alanna continues on her spiritual journey, as do we all, and I continue to pray for her peace and her protection. I am encouraged to know that on the other side of the country, my daughter is rediscovering Mass and the peace of eucharistic adoration. Her eyes are healed and I pray that her hurts will one day be as well. It's said that true devotion to Our Lady always leads to her Son. On my first trip to Medjugorje, Our Lady revealed herself to me in a special and spectacular way. This was a great blessing that I will treasure for the rest of my life. But even more magnificent than that heavenly vision, the Blessed Mother showed me something far greater: her Son in the Blessed Sacrament.

Joanne Zabielski, New York

"Dear children! Today, I invite you to fall in love with the most holy sacrament of the altar. Adore him, little children, in your parishes and in this way you will be united with the entire world. Jesus will become your friend and you will not talk of Him like someone whom you barely know. Unity with Him will be a joy for you and you will become witnesses to the love of Jesus that He has for every creature. Little children, when you adore Jesus you are also close to me. Thank you for having responded to my call."

Message of September 25, 1995

Confession

*"Dear children! I invite you
to open the door of your heart to Jesus as
the flower opens itself to the sun. Jesus desires to
fill your hearts with peace and joy. You cannot, little
children, realize peace if you are not at peace with Jesus.
Therefore, I invite you to Confession so Jesus may be your
truth and peace. So, little children, pray to have the strength
to realize what I am telling you. I am with you and I love
you. Thank you for having responded to my call."*
Message of January 25, 1995

10
A New Game Plan

Sometimes God, the ultimate quarterback, calls a surprising play in our lives. I was certain (as was everyone else who ever knew me) that I would be wearing a uniform after college—that is, a pro-football uniform. Well, I am in a uniform all right, but not the one we had all imagined. I've traded my football pads for a Roman collar and it's the best decision I've ever made.

I was spoon-fed my Catholic faith by my dad, a convert, and my mom, a daily communicant from the time she was seven years old. The Church has always been an important part of my family's life. It was not uncommon for priests to come to our home for Thanksgiving, Christmas, or just to play "Schmear," a popular card game in Oconto, Wisconsin, where I grew up. My family owned a restaurant, so I grew up in a public environment, getting to know people and serve them. As the youngest of six children, I attended Catholic schools from first grade through sixth and then attended public middle and high school because there was no higher Catholic education offered in my hometown.

I was never what you would call a small child. By eighth grade, at six foot three and 286 pounds, I was bigger than my teachers were. The varsity football coach of the high school approached my parents and asked them for permission to bring me up to the varsity football team. By the time I was a freshman, I had lettered in three varsity sports and continued through high school on a successful sports track. In my senior year, I earned a full football scholarship to Eastern Michigan University, an NCAA Division I school in Ypsilanti. It was during my college years when my faith struggle began to happen. I was playing football and majoring in art education, but I was alone for the first time and without the support of my family or friends. I was very lonely, and because of that I started drinking and smoking marijuana.

In my junior year, my mom figured out that I was in trouble and asked me to go with her to Medjugorje, where she served as a tour guide. I agreed to go with her over Christmas break in 1994, but I did not go with an open heart. In fact, I was pretty resistant to the whole idea. My mom wanted me to make a confession in Medjugorje, telling me that if I couldn't go for myself, at least do it for her. My mom is a pretty persuasive individual. I said the first real prayer in my life in Medjugorje when I was walking one day in the vineyards below Mt. Krizevac. Basically, I gave God an ultimatum. I challenged His existence by saying, "Lord, if You exist, I don't know You. You could be the biggest con artist this world has ever seen. I have no proof of You; I've never seen You; I've never felt You. I just don't know You exist." I told God I would go to the sacrament of Reconciliation as my mom had asked, but I wanted Him to prove to me that He existed. "If You don't," I told Him, "I'm done with religion."

About thirty minutes later, I was in the confessional where I gave up about four years of sinfulness to an American priest. During the words of absolution, I felt the physical presence of Christ, although I could not see Him. Suddenly, something pierced my chest and it felt as if something were violently ripped out of me, to the point where I screamed aloud. My first conscious thought was "Oh my God, You *are* real!" I started crying and I wept for about forty-five minutes because of my sinfulness and unworthiness. My penance was to say five Our Fathers and it took me almost an hour to do this because as I prayed, pictures of people I had hurt in my life—especially the women I had dated—flashed through my mind.

An hour later, I was attending the English Mass and sitting in the choir loft at St. James Church. Throughout the Mass, I kept reliving that moment in the confessional. When I finally came to a sense of awareness, the priest was starting his homily. I said my second conscious prayer. "Lord, let me open my heart to what this priest has to say." At that moment I had my second mystical experience. I recognize it today as a Pentecostal experience, but I didn't know it at the time. The Holy Spirit anointed me in a power greater than any drug, any sexual experience, or any sports victory. In fact, if you combined the best of these and multiplied that by infinity, you still couldn't touch this experience. I was afraid to open my eyes because I thought I was levitating. The sensation lasted for about twenty minutes. When I went outside after the Mass, a woman who apparently had witnessed what I had experienced asked me to pray over her. I'd never been asked this question before, and when I did, she went limp and rested in the Spirit. ["Resting in" or "being slain in" the Spirit means being overwhelmed with the presence of God after being prayed over. Many people are overwhelmed to the point of physical weakness and they fall down.] I was quite shaken by this and very much afraid. I didn't understand any of it.

Six months later, my mom asked me to return to Medjugorje for the fourteenth anniversary of the apparitions. I was getting close to finishing college and this time I was eager to go. On the second day there, we went to hear Father Jozo speak. Being a little more familiar with the process, I decided to go up and help catch people that were falling down after being prayed over by the priests. I was following an old Capuchin priest and he was working me pretty hard because he had "dropped" about a hundred people. Eventually he came to a woman in a wheelchair. While he was talking with her, the woman's husband told me that his wife had been in a car accident seven years prior, which completely severed her spinal cord. Since then, she had not moved a muscle in her legs and they were severely atrophied. I figured the case was hopeless. The old Capuchin priest continued to pray over the woman, blessing her knees, ankles, and hips for about forty minutes. Seeing his diligence, I decided I probably should start praying for her too, so I offered up a rather flippant prayer asking God to show us His power by getting this woman on her feet. For the first time, I heard Christ speak to me. He said, *"If I get her out of the wheelchair, will you enter the seminary?"* My response was immediate. "Absolutely not," I said. "That's too easy for You." A few minutes passed and I watched the priest continuing his efforts. I reapproached God internally. I said, "If you get her out of this wheelchair and walk her around the entire church (which was a rather large building), then I will enter the seminary." Within five seconds, the woman was up on her feet without anyone's assistance. She began to walk, pushing her wheelchair all around the church, past the tabernacle, and back to the point where she started. All I could manage to utter were a few expletives and walk out of the church.

God could not have picked a worse time to present a career change. Football scouts were beginning to look at me. I had an excellent shot at the NFL, and God wanted to intercept that plan *now?* It was a difficult time for me, to say the least. I returned to school and continued playing ball, trying to sort things out. The last game of my college football career was played against Ball State University. During the game, I had a very strong déjà vu experience in which I seemed to know what was going to happen before it actually happened. I didn't understand this phenomenon; it was very strange and frightening. We ended up winning the game and while the guys celebrated afterward in the locker room, I drifted off to a corner by myself, put a towel over my head, and cried silently. I thought I was going crazy.

That night my football roommates had a party at our house. I went to my room around midnight, prayed the Rosary, and then went to bed. At 3:00 a.m., I awoke from a vivid dream about football in which I was playing the same ten plays as our last game. God revealed to me that I had dreamed this dream as a child. It's a fact that whenever anyone asked me as a kid what I wanted to be when I grew up, I would always say I was going to play in the NFL. It occurred to me at that moment that our Eastern Michigan college uniforms were exactly the same as the Philadelphia Eagles, and Ball State's uniforms were exactly the same as the Phoenix Cardinals, two professional teams I grew up watching on television. In response to this realization God said to me, *"You have fulfilled your dream. Now fulfill Mine: priesthood."* At that moment, I made the decision to finish school and start looking seriously for a seminary.

My mom was elated about my surprising announcement, but the rest of the family could not understand it at first. They suggested I play ball for a few years first and then enter the seminary. But I knew this was not to be. Today my family is very supportive of my vocation, but back then it was a hardship for them. My friends didn't understand my choice, either. Many people were shocked, especially old girlfriends. I endured a great deal of emotional persecution and ridicule.

After finishing my degree and working for six months as a substitute teacher for kindergarten through high school, I interviewed with the Diocese of Green Bay about the priesthood. Green Bay sent me to Mundelein Seminary in Chicago to be interviewed. I wasn't planning to bring up my Medjugorje conversion, but the board evidently had heard about it. They asked me to describe my experience there. I was then asked if I didn't receive the gift of healing when I became a priest, would I quit the priesthood? I quickly but respectfully pointed out that all priests have the gift of healing because every time they forgive sins in the confessional they are healing people spiritually. Nonetheless, I was not accepted at Mundelein.

Discouraged, I considered being a walk-on for the Green Bay Packers tryouts. But I knew I couldn't make this decision without praying about it first. God answered my prayer by making me aware of Bishop James Sullivan of Fargo, North Dakota, who was known to have a strong Marian devotion. When I spoke with him, Bishop Sullivan asked me how soon I could get to Fargo; school started on Tuesday. And so I started minor seminary formation without even filling out an application to a diocese. From Fargo, I continued studies at Mount Saint Mary's seminary in Emmitsburg, Maryland.

Seminary life was a bit challenging for me. Most seminarians receive a quiet call to the priesthood. They get a notion that they might be called to a religious life and then they pursue that idea, growing in holiness as they grow in formation. Perhaps later on in priesthood they might experience something miraculous. For a handful of seminarians I have encountered and for myself, we seem to be going through the process backward. The miraculous happened first. God intervened in our lives and then we found ourselves going through the seminary education system to try and figure out what exactly happened to us, and what we were supposed to do with it.

When the time came to write my petition for diaconate to the bishop of Fargo, I was feeling some anxiety about it. It was not about the call to priesthood—I knew for certain that God had called me to that. But I was doing an internship at the time for the diocese at a very rural parish and I was feeling lonely for my family back home. What I really wanted to do was serve God closer to my home in Wisconsin. I contacted my bishop in Fargo and told him of my concerns. He was very sympathetic as his home was in Denver, and he gave me permission to make some inquiries elsewhere. Once again, I went to God in prayer. "If it is Your will that I be ordained in Fargo, so be it. I will do that. But if You want me to consider the archdiocese of Milwaukee, I need proof. I need to have the archbishop himself call me and then I'll know for sure." On the second day after that prayer, the archbishop of Milwaukee called me. Through a mutual priest friend he had heard about my desire to return home. To make the transfer meant that I would have to turn down ordination in Fargo and resign, submit myself to the diocese of Milwaukee, and take a two-year delay. This is exactly what I did. God opened the door, and I walked through.

I am confident today in my spirituality and in what God is capable of doing because of all the amazing things He has revealed to me. I think my confidence and my large size may give people a wrong impression of arrogance, but that is not the case at all. My confidence is not in myself, but in God. I have the utmost faith that if we ask something that is within His will, He will provide for us. This mentality overflows in my ministry. My hope as a new priest is that I can help people discern their gifts in order to help the mission of the Church and likewise deepen their relationship with God. If I could achieve anything in my priesthood, it would be to show people God's love as He demonstrated it to me in that confessional in Medjugorje. Not surprisingly, Confession remains a very important part of my life. I have had a spiritual director since the time of my conversion and I have found that allowing someone else to help me discern different aspects of my vocation has been very fruitful indeed.

For me, Medjugorje is about adoration, the sacraments, and the Church. After twenty-five years of daily messages, theologians have still not found any contradictions to scripture in the heavenly words imparted there. The messages coincide perfectly with the Gospels. Since I have accepted God's invitation to the priesthood, as revealed to me in Medjugorje, my faith life has been a joy. I particularly have enjoyed working with young people through numerous years of youth ministry. Some of the kids look at me, a tough right tackle turned gentle priest, and see a hero. Others look at me and see a fool. But I guess if I had to choose I would rather be a fool...for Christ.

Father Michael Lightner, Wisconsin

"Dear children! Today I call you, through prayer and sacrifice, to prepare yourselves for the coming of the Holy Spirit. Little children, this is a time of grace and so, again, I call you to decide for God the creator. Allow Him to transform and change you. May your heart be prepared to listen to, and live, everything that the Holy Spirit has in His plan for each of you. Little children, allow the Holy Spirit to lead you on the way of truth and salvation towards eternal life. Thank you for having responded to my call." Message of May 25, 1998

11
Meeting People Where They Are

I grew up in a Catholic-Protestant home where religion was the biggest reason my parents fought. My mother was raised Catholic and my father had joined an Assembly of God church, where he became very condemning of Catholicism. As a child, I grew up confused. For the most part, I sided with my dad because of the fear he instilled in me that Catholics were in great danger of going to hell.

It was my Croatian Catholic grandmother who first told me about Medjugorje when I was about eight or nine years old. She had a strong devotion to Our Blessed Mother and prayed the Rosary often. My grandmother had never been to Medjugorje but she had friends who traveled there. When she would tell me the stories of the children seeing the Virgin, there was a part of me that wanted to believe in it, but Marian devotion was a "bad thing" according to my father, so I didn't really take it to heart.

My grandmother passed away when I was sixteen and it marked the beginning of a dark period in my life. By the time I was college bound, my life had taken a pretty dangerous path. I began to get heavily involved with drugs and alcohol, mostly as a coping mechanism for a lot of the unresolved pain I had been dealing with as a kid. School was something I was good at—it was the one coping mechanism that worked for me—but when that failed my expectations, I began to use drugs and alcohol even more. I wanted nothing to do with Jesus because I saw Him as the reason my parents fought so much. He also received my blame for the war in Bosnia that I was studying in history class. To me, religion was something that got in the way of people being good to one another. The more I turned my back on faith, the more dependent I became on chemicals and bad relationships.

From the outside, things looked good. I was an over-achiever, finishing college with bachelor's degrees in English and history by the time I was twenty. But on the inside, my life was falling apart. I had fallen in love with a guy who I thought was the answer to all my problems, but that was turning out to be a dead end, too. I figured I could go to graduate school, although I had no idea what I wanted to do. In my younger life I had dabbled in music and theater and really enjoyed it, but my father had convinced me that my talent was mediocre and that I could never really do anything with it. So here I was at twenty, feeling old and as though I had missed my opportunity to do anything with my life.

Prior to starting graduate school as a history major in the fall of 2000, I planned a six-week backpacking trip by myself through Europe. Traveling was something I had always enjoyed and I wanted to see more of Eastern Europe before I began studying it. I had been to Croatia twice because I have family there and I was interested in seeing that part of the world. So I donned my backpack and drifted somewhat aimlessly through Eastern Europe. Still, deep in my heart, I found myself searching for something more—there seemed to be some sort of spiritual craving awakening within me.

The second place I visited on my trip was Czestochowa, a huge Marian shrine in Poland. There is a famous image of Our Lady there painted by St. Luke the Evangelist. The legend says that while he painted this image the Blessed Mother told him the story of Jesus, which he later incorporated into his Gospel. From there I traveled to Krakow, two hours away, and found myself on the town square one night for a concert. As fate would have it, I met a group of eight American missionaries, unaffiliated with any religious denomination, doing humanitarian aid work in Czestochowa. This proved to be a significant meeting for me because, for the first time in my life, I was being accepted and related to by total strangers when I began asking questions about faith. These people were my age. They were in love with the Lord, but they were cool; they were normal. Up until that point, my encounters with "holy people" involved Bible-thumpers like my dad or casual Catholics like people at my mom's parish. I found myself irresistibly drawn to these young Americans. I hung out with them that night in Krakow and traveled to Czestochowa with them the next day. That night I stayed at the mission where they were working and we prayed together. I asked more questions, telling them that I hated denominations because of what I had seen happen to my parents. They said that was okay; I didn't need to worry about that right now; I just needed to focus on Jesus. To me, this was critical. These Americans met me where I was, emotionally and spiritually. They didn't tell me I was doing anything wrong. They didn't condemn me. That night, they helped me understand that Jesus was real, and it all happened in the shadow of a major shrine of Our Lady.

The next day I went to Mass for the first time in ages and it started to feel so right. Three weeks later, I ended up in Medjugorje. I hadn't planned to go there originally. Recalling my grandmother's stories about the children and the visions, I thought I could stop there for one night and pick up some rosaries to bring back as souvenirs. So I took the bus in from Sarajevo. As soon as I stepped out onto the soil, I felt an overwhelming conviction that whatever was happening here was real. I was sure of it. There are no words to describe this feeling I had; I just knew.

I got a room at the first place I could find so that I could unpack. Next I went to one of the gift shops and picked up a general guidebook about the apparitions, because now that I had a sense that this was real, I wanted to know exactly what was happening here. To me, what was most convincing were the messages the Blessed Mother was delivering in Medjugorje. She was talking about peace, joy, and loving each other. She was meeting people where they were and inviting them to come closer to God's love.

The next morning I attended Mass and heard a homily that seemed to be directed especially to me. The priest was talking about young people who had fallen away from faith and he was inviting them to come back. He didn't tell us to come back; he invited us. This priest exhibited love in a way I had never experienced from an ordained person. For the first time, I began to realize that things were going to be all right. I had solidified the presence of Jesus in my life.

I ended up staying in Medjugorje three nights. Most of the time was spent in quiet prayer by myself. Then I finished up my backpacking trip and returned home with my souvenirs. The experience of Medjugorje had a great impact on me, but I wasn't out of the woods yet. I started graduate school and soon was completely miserable, which escalated my drug use to a dangerous level. I realized the man that I was in love with was not going to love me the way I wanted him to, and at the same time I was confronting both of my parents about a number of issues from the past. Remarkably, during all of this turbulence, I continued to go to Mass and pray my Rosary. Still, I was unable to shake the depression.

On Thanksgiving night I went out and got "obliterated" with some friends. I wasn't actively trying to kill myself, but I was using drugs so much that I didn't care if I died. When I woke up Friday morning, I suddenly knew that I had to get out of there or I would be dead by Christmas. It became clear to me: *go to Medjugorje.* I wrestled in my mind about what I would do there, but I at least had the ability to speak Croatian. At the very least, I could spend a few months there to get myself better from the depression and the drug use. It wasn't that I was looking for a miraculous cure. I just had the feeling that somehow I would meet the right people in Medjugorje and that I could rehabilitate myself there.

That same Friday morning was the day I would later discover that Father Slavko Barbaric had passed away. Father Slavko was a very holy Franciscan priest who served in Medjugorje from the earliest days of the apparitions. Through his books and homilies and his example of humility and love, Father Slavko touched many people and taught them to open their hearts to Jesus and Mary. Unfortunately I never had a chance to meet this man, but I would end up working on three of his major projects in Medjugorje. I tell people with conviction today that I honestly believe I was the first life Father Slavko saved when he got to heaven.

In any case, I didn't tell anyone where I was going except my brother—it was that desperate a situation. I knew that if I told my mom or my friends, they would try and talk me into finding help at home. But I needed distance. So I packed my things, wrote detailed notes for everyone and left that Monday, intending to stay in Medjugorje for at least six weeks. I ended up living there for two and a half years.

One of the first things I did in Medjugorje was make my first confession in about nine years with a priest who turned out to be a recovering alcoholic. I didn't have to explain about addiction to this priest. He understood fully and was able to give me some excellent guidance. I saw this as a sign that God was taking care of me already. That priest was the first of a long line of people I believe God intended me to meet to help me in my healing. This process took time. It wasn't as if I went to Medjugorje and in six weeks I was better. It took the entire two and a half years before I finally figured out what this whole conversion thing was about.

At first I went through a zealous post-conversion phase in which I was determined to be the best Catholic I could be, and I found myself criticizing those whom I judged were not. I started getting caught up in this idea that you had to follow the exact schedule of fasting and prayers or you wouldn't get to heaven. In a way, I was becoming the Bible-thumper that my dad was, and that thought terrified me. This wasn't evangelization. Evangelization was what those kids I met in Poland had been doing: loving people, not judging them.

One of the most significant persons I met in Medjugorje was a woman named Janet. She had been to Medjugorje many times to do humanitarian aid work during the war, and I learned that she was coming over to start an Alcoholics Anonymous (AA) meeting in Bosnia. Janet ended up being the counseling presence I needed to put my life back on track. She helped me to integrate the spirituality I had found with the work that God wanted me to do in myself. She had a beautiful sense of the messages and how to implement God's will in very practical ways. Janet showed me that being a Rosary-thumper was not the way to "get" people. What was required was to carry the love of

Jesus in one's heart and encounter people at their level of spiritual awareness.

Not long after my arrival in Medjugorje, I sought work in the community. I saw that as a fitting way of putting Our Lady's messages into action. The first job I got was at Mother's Village, a children's home for the orphans of the war founded by Father Slavko. Father Svetozar Kraljevic, the main English-speaking priest there, was aware of my ability to speak Croatian. He gave me the job of teaching English to the children at Mother's Village. Working with wounded children helped me to experience God's love at work. A lot of my own healing started in this place because I could connect with these kids. They, in turn, taught me important lessons such as how to accept and love people no matter what.

In addition to that work, I also began coordinating music for the English Mass. My job was to be the song leader or assist the visiting priests to make sure they had everything they needed in terms of music for their liturgies. I met about five hundred priests in that job and I often ended up talking with them afterward about theology and spirituality. One priest, Father Ciaran McDonnell from Ireland, had a tremendous influence on me. He came on sabbatical to live in Medjugorje for nine months and help with the English-speaking pilgrims. Father Ciaran had been a musician in a rock band before becoming a priest and he taught me how to play the guitar. He saw in me a gift and he really worked with me on my music. That was one of the biggest blessings for me about Medjugorje: it put me back in touch with the music I had been away from for so long.

In the beginning of 2002, at the request of many pilgrims, I made a compact disc (CD) called "Give Us Your Peace." It was a small, independent production for the benefit of charity work in Bosnia, but it had big results. What I like most about this recording is that it brought together twenty musicians from nine different countries and was recorded in Medjugorje, where each of us had had special spiritual experiences. Being able to work with musicians from around the world—as their equal—gave me the confirmation I needed that this was what I should be doing.

Late that fall, Father Svetozar pulled me aside and told me it was time I thought about returning home. He said he thought I could do more for people by living outside of Medjugorje. He wanted me to go back to school to get my master's degree and suggested Franciscan University in Steubenville, Ohio, which is like Medjugorje in America. I didn't know how to take this at first, because I was feeling so useful here. I ran this by Janet and she concurred. She suggested I look into the counseling program there because she saw how well I worked with kids and knew I could understand the pain of others.

And so a new chapter in my life began. I returned to the United States and applied and was accepted into the master's degree counseling program at Steubenville. With my musical interest very much alive, I produced a CD and stage production entitled "Children of Life," a pro-life musical that was performed in Youngstown. I also provided music for the local televised Mass, which I loved, with a fellow musician named Jim Stafford. It was Jim who introduced me to a whole new type of music that would once again change my life: alternative country. This music features country instruments and songs that speak more deeply to the human experience of joy and sorrow. Essentially, it is secular music with a spiritual slant. To me, this was a way to reach people who would not ordinarily be drawn to pure Christian music.

With the spiritual poverty I saw in my home country, I really felt called to this new sound.

As part of my master's degree in counseling, I did an internship at a hospital, where I worked with hard-core troubled youth, most of them with criminal records and many of them victims of serious abuse. I found that these kids were receptive to the kind of music I was now writing. They could relate to it. In my counseling experience, I've found that meeting people on their level, dealing with their hurt, and showing them love helps them to be more receptive to hearing about faith later on. As it says in St. Paul's letter to the Corinthians, "I gave you milk to drink, not solid food; for you were not yet able to receive it."

My counseling and music continue to harmonize today. I wrote a song about my grandfather's life and death, and how it affected me. People in coffeehouses would come up to me afterward and talk to me about their experience of grief and loss. It's amazing, but I'm doing more ministry work playing out in secular venues than I ever did in church settings. My grandfather's illness and death brings this story full circle. When I moved back to the United States in May 2003, my mother suggested that I live with my grandfather since he was sick with cancer and needed help, and I needed room and board. So I went to live in the house where my Croatian grandmother had once told me her stories. And there I had a most pleasant surprise. Among her many Marian objects, still left in the same place since the time of her passing, I discovered a number of items from Medjugorje. They were all over the house, but I had never noticed before. As a firm believer in the intercessory prayer of the saints, I believe that my grandmother's prayers were a huge factor in leading me to Medjugorje and helping to get my life turned around—the prayers of my grandmother, and Father Slavko.

When people ask if I believe in the miracles that are routinely reported in Medjugorje, I tell them I absolutely do. But do I think that's what Medjugorje is all about? Not at all. People are surprised that I lived there for more than two years and never once saw the sun spin. I suppose I never needed to; I saw what happened in my own life, and that's spinning sun enough for me. When I think about the people I've met in Medjugorje and how much they taught me, I wouldn't trade a single one of them to see my rosary turn gold. Their friendship and ability to show me what conversion is all about is all the gold I will ever need.

Medjugorje gave me the clarity I needed when I was visionless. It prepared me for a vocation as counselor and musician so that I can bring the messages of peace and reconciliation to a world that desperately needs to hear it— right where they are.

Jamie Marich, Ohio

"Dear children, today I rejoice with you and I invite you to open yourselves to me, and become an instrument in my hands, for the salvation of the world. I desire, little children, that all of you who have felt the fragrance of holiness, through these messages which I am giving you, to carry it in this world, hungry for God and God's love. I thank you all for having responded in such a number and I bless you all with my motherly blessing. Thank you for having responded to my call!" Message of March 25, 1994

12
River of Love

As a child, I was brought up in a Catholic Croatian home in California where faith was a central part of our lives. We went to Mass regularly as a family and celebrated the sacrament of Reconciliation every month as a normal and natural part of my upbringing. I can remember my sister and me pretending to have Masses in the house and trying to recite the prayers we heard in church. I also remember draping a cloth over my head and pretending to be a nun. My uncle, who was a priest, must have seen something in my young religious fervor, because he frequently brought me little gifts of Bibles or prayer books when he came to visit.

This religious fervor, unfortunately, did not last. Later in my teens, I didn't really pray all that much and I found it difficult to go to Mass. I went to Confession far less frequently and more so out of obligation than desire. God just wasn't a big part of my life any longer. At twenty, I chose a spouse without any prayerful discernment and the marriage was terrible and emotionally abusive from the beginning. I stayed in it primarily for Katie and Stephen, the two beautiful children we had together, but my family finally convinced me in time to take the children and move out of the house. Not long after, my husband and I were divorced.

As a single mom, life was difficult and I had to live on welfare for a time. I made things particularly hard for myself because I did not turn to God or the Church for support. But

God did not abandon me. Deep in my soul, He had planted a little ray of hope some years before, in 1981, when I first learned of a miracle that was happening in Medjugorje. This village was not far from several of my Croatian relatives, and one of them had actually been healed there. From the first time I heard about the apparitions, I believed. Perhaps I was open to the idea because of the movie *Song of Bernadette* that I had loved as a child. If it could happen in Lourdes, I thought, why not in my homeland? In 1983, shortly before the breakup of my marriage, I had an opportunity to visit Medjugorje during a trip to see my relatives. In those days there was not much to see or do, and there was very little information about what was happening there. St. James Church was surrounded by dirt and police barricades and the mountains were off limits to people by orders of the Communist government. Still, I had a warm feeling in my heart about this place, a feeling of being home. It wasn't until months later when I read the book *The Apparitions of Our Lady at Medjugorje* by Father Svetozar Kraljevic that I began to realize the magnitude of this event. I desired with all my heart to return one day.

In the subsequent years, I tried to follow the news of Medjugorje as it became available, but information was slow in coming. As I learned of the messages and what Our Lady was calling us to do, I made some attempts to try and incorporate them into my life, stumbling as I went along. My next opportunity to go to Medjugorje came in 1991 and this time I experienced the fullness, beauty, and wonder of this holy place, by witnessing powerful worship, spiritual conversions, physical healings, and supernatural events. It was a most profound pilgrimage and it broke my heart to have to leave. I felt an overwhelming pull to return, even stronger than before, and the following year I went again. After that, I began to take family and friends with me on pilgrimages there.

Because I had learned to speak Croatian as a child, I was able to meet the locals, including the visionaries, and ask them many questions about the history and details of the apparitions. I also read everything available on the subject. My life was filled with joy as I began to truly live the messages. My prayer life deepened, the Mass and scripture became alive for me, and Confession showed me areas in my life where I needed to make changes, just as Our Lady said. My peace and joy spread to my children, who at a young age began to join me in prayer and fasting, of their own volition. Still, I couldn't help thinking how wonderful it would be to share this experience with someone special. But I worried about whether I would ever find a man that would want to pray the Rosary, go to daily Mass and monthly Confession, and read scripture with me. I remembered reading somewhere that if more people prayed about finding the right spouse, there wouldn't be so many divorces. Therefore, for the next two years, I prayed for this intention. I didn't want to repeat the mistake of picking someone out by myself, so I asked Our Lady to intercede for me by granting me two signs that would help me recognize the man that was chosen for me by God. The first sign I asked for was the gift of a rosary, to show me that this man had a love for the Blessed Mother. The second sign I requested was the gift of a crucifix, so I would know this man loved God. Since these items are not typically something a man would give a woman, I thought they would be a good test.

In 1995, my brother gave me a computer. I taught myself how to use the Internet, which was in its infancy back then. My first interest was to find out more information about

Medjugorje, but I could not find any Web sites about it. I entertained the thought of creating one myself, but my computer skills were lacking. Eventually I discovered a site called "Apparitions of the Virgin Mary in Medjugorje." I was impressed with how much information was posted on this site, but I was also concerned whether the Webmaster was using reliable sources. At the bottom of the site was a name, Steve Shawl, and I sent an e-mail congratulating him on his work and inquiring where he got his information.

The next day I received a long response from Steve detailing his sources, which were all credible. I offered to share some information for his Web site that I had gathered through my numerous trips to Medjugorje and my relationships with the visionaries and the Franciscans. Through our ongoing e-mail communication, I soon discovered that Steve was a special individual. He shared with me his own story of conversion, how he had fallen away from the faith as a young person and how he first found out about Medjugorje through Wayne Weible's newspaper, given to him by his father. Steve was skeptical at first about the whole thing, wondering if it were true, why wasn't it in every newspaper? But it intrigued him enough to continue reading about it and the more he read, the more he believed. The turning point for him was a very personal experience he had in which he truly felt the presence of Our Lady in front of him. He could feel the incredible love and grace of the Blessed Mother in his heart and it literally transformed his faith in an instant. Steve told me that Our Lady spoke to him in his heart, asking him to help spread the messages of Medjugorje through the Internet. While Steve owned a computer business, he knew nothing about the Internet because it was so new. He answered Our Lady out loud by saying, "Blessed Mother, if this is not my imagination, and if this is truly what you are asking of me, you have to make it happen, because I have no idea how to do this." Quickly, his prayer was answered. One thing led to another and Steve was able to learn the computer language necessary to create a Web site and have it up and running within three months. As a result of his intense experience with Our Lady, Steve returned to the Church after more than twenty years and made a heartfelt confession. He began to live the messages immediately, including fasting on Wednesdays and Fridays. His deepening love for Our Lady triggered a simultaneous yearning for the Eucharist and all the sacraments of the Church.

The more I learned about Steve, the more certain I became that he was the man I had been praying for. Still, I waited for my signs. A few weeks later, I was offered a partnership in a brand new company. The pay was good, but I knew the hours would be long. It would also require moving and putting the kids in a new school and having to use a daycare center as well. Most of my family and friends tried to convince me to take this position, but I was worried that if I did, there would be no hope of anything happening between Steve, who lived in Illinois, and me.

When I wrote to Steve about the job offer, his response astounded me. He shared candidly that he had been praying novenas and Chaplets of Divine Mercy to find a woman with whom he could spend the rest of his life. He told me that he had asked the Blessed Mother for two signs to confirm when he had found this woman and that I had fulfilled his two signs. I was completely blown away by this and told Steve that I had also prayed for two signs, but they were yet to be fulfilled. Plus, I had to consult my children about the matter. When I sat down and talked with them, they were completely supportive of my pursuing this relationship. Now that I had their blessing, I had to wait on the Blessed Mother.

Later that night, I was praying and asking with all my heart if Steve was the man that I was supposed to marry. A thought suddenly occurred to me that just the day before, Steve had sent rosaries to my children and me. I talked to him the next day and told him I had received my first sign, but I still had one to go before I would know for sure. Steve told me later that after our conversation, he went to Mass and prayed a Rosary, asking the Blessed Mother to reveal what my second sign was. Apparently, he got his answer, because he wrote back and told me that he knew without a doubt what my second sign was: he was to send me a crucifix. When I confessed that it was my second sign, we knew for certain that God had a special reason for us being a family. I flew to Illinois to meet him and confirmed our suspicions.

A few weeks later, Steve went to Medjugorje with his father for the first time. I wasn't able to speak with him while he was there, but I held him close in prayer. One night, as I prayed, I had a sort of dream or vision that Steve and I and the children were together in Medjugorje in front of the Blessed Mother. We were hugging, and all of a sudden there was a great white light that came and fused us together as a family. It was such a wonderful feeling. To my amazement, when Steve returned from Medjugorje he told me that he had the exact same dream.

Steve and I, together with my family, traveled to Medjugorje in 1996 for the fifteenth anniversary of the apparitions. There he proposed to me, at the foot of the cross on top of Mt. Krizevac. A year later we were married, holding in our hands the crucifix that he had sent me, which is the tradition in Croatian weddings. Our wedding took place in Illinois, where the children and I had relocated after our engagement, and we renewed our wedding vows in Medjugorje with a big reception for all of my relatives. To further bless and solidify our marriage, God gave us a precious little girl named Tihana Maria.

During the time of our engagement and preparation for marriage, the Web site, which was renamed the "Medjugorje Web" had become quite comprehensive with a growing readership. I suggested to Steve that we sponsor an annual pilgrimage to Medjugorje and this turned out to be quite successful. Soon people wanted to go more than once a year and we started having two pilgrimages. When that wasn't enough, we moved to monthly trips, and today we do two per month, with Steve or me serving as tour guide. As demand for pilgrimages increased, Steve's computer company began to go bankrupt, which was confirmation to the two of us that this was to be our full-time ministry.

Our mission with the Web site is to help people stay up-to-date with the messages and developments in Medjugorje and to maintain their faith and fervor in order to live and spread the messages. Today the Medjugorje Web is one of the most frequented sites on the subject, having attracted a total of nearly thirty million visitors. We have an e-mail list of more than 75,000 subscribers from all over the world who receive the latest message and its commentary by the Franciscans as soon as it becomes available to us from the parish in Medjugorje. Many of our subscribers are responsible for Marian Centers and Medjugorje prayer groups, and they in turn spread the messages to their organizations.

In addition to current messages and commentaries, our Web site features archived messages with a concordance to enable people to look up messages based on a specific word.

We also provide information on the history of Medjugorje and the visionaries; organizations, conferences, and other programs in Medjugorje; Marian conferences in the United States; and pilgrimage information. To meet the increasing demand for rosaries, books, music, statues, and other materials related to Medjugorje, we have created the Franciscan-MIR bookstore to offer these products on-line.

An important fruit of the Medjugorje Web is the Queen of Peace Internet International Prayer Group (IIPG) that was started in 1999. The idea was originally conceived by Nedjo Brecic, a good and holy man and a member of Ivan's Medjugorje prayer group, which Our Lady asked Ivan (a visionary) to create in 1982. With the growing interest of pilgrims to stay in touch with this prayer group, Nedjo felt called to invite the world to join through use of the Internet, but he wasn't sure quite how to accomplish this. With my ability to translate and Steve's computer knowledge, we helped Nedjo establish a Web site under his name just in time for the seventeenth anniversary of the prayer group. Nedjo was never happier than on this particular day; therefore, it was a great shock to all of us that immediately following the apparition that night, he peacefully passed away. We have kept the prayer group as Nedjo envisioned—a place to discuss the messages and support one another in living and spreading them. What started as a group of sixty people today consists of more than twenty-five hundred members from all over the world, not all of whom are Catholic. With the help of five other moderators, we guide discussions to keep them on topic and also post prayer requests and commentaries by priests. Often we hear stories about people joining the faith or returning

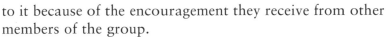

to it because of the encouragement they receive from other members of the group.

For Steve and me, Medjugorje is a way of life. We choose to live simply and while we will never be rich, we have abundance where it counts: in joy and service to Our Lady and to her Son. The amount of travel we do can be difficult at times on our family, but all of us are committed to living and spreading the messages and answering people's questions and concerns about Medjugorje. The hard work is well worth the graces and blessings of being able to witness first-hand how lives are changed and improved by the messages of these apparitions. Our Lady has asked all of us to live her messages with love, and to transmit them to the whole world so that a river of love flows to people who are full of hatred and without peace. Steve and I pray that our Web site can be a part of that river, flowing out into the spiritual deserts in this world and setting all the captives free.

Ana and Steve Shawl, Illinois

"Dear children! Today I invite you to become missionaries of my messages, which I am giving here through this place that is dear to me. God has allowed me to stay this long with you, and therefore, little children, I invite you to live with love the messages I give and to transmit them to the whole world, so that a river of love flows to people who are full of hatred and without peace. I invite you, little children, to become peace where there is no peace and light where there is darkness, so that each heart accepts the light and the way of salvation. Thank you for having responded to my call."
Message of February 25, 1995

13
A Signpost for God

My parents were practicing Catholics who took our family to Mass every Sunday and participated in various ministries in the parish. Like many Catholic families, we prayed grace before meals, had numerous religious items around our home, and were encouraged to abstain during Lent. However, I did not have much personal zeal for the Catholic faith. I attended public school most of my youth and did not learn a great deal in religious education, which ended after my Confirmation in the eighth grade. As a result, my spirituality was not well-developed growing up and I knew very little about the substance of my faith.

During my high school and college years, it is fair to say that I was shaped more by society than by the Gospel of Jesus Christ. My high school friends and I spoke often of our plans for success and accumulating wealth; our desire to make money was fueled by having parents who were entrepreneurs. I had a particular interest in real estate investment and planned on being a millionaire before the age of thirty. To give me a basis for my future, I pursued the study of accounting and business at Purdue University.

As a youth, I went to church with my parents simply because it was expected of me. When I left for Purdue, however, it was a different story. Because of my ignorance of the Mass and the Eucharist, and my dislike of the 1970s liturgical style at the campus Newman Center, I seldom went to church. I did,

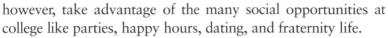

however, take advantage of the many social opportunities at college like parties, happy hours, dating, and fraternity life.

Despite my secular frame of mind, there was one part of my childhood spirituality that was ingrained in me, and that was my attitude toward Lent. My parents did a good job of instilling in their children a healthy understanding of abstinence in order (with God's grace) to affect a positive change in our lives. They encouraged us not to simply give up something out of obligation or habit, but to pray and ask God to work in and through us during this time. During my years at Purdue, this understanding kept me connected to the Lord. I prayed daily and among other sacrifices gave up drinking alcohol, which was a central part of many social functions. Looking back, I think that God was desperately trying to become a larger part of my life, inspiring my willingness to be obedient, strengthening my will power, and preparing me for what would happen in my future.

After graduation, I became a Certified Public Accountant (CPA), and began working at a large accounting firm where I met another young entrepreneur who would become a good friend and business partner. He shared my interest in real estate investment and soon we purchased our first building together with creative financing, including cash advances on credit cards. After ten months of renovation, we sold it for a significant profit. Life was going exactly as planned.

At about this time, in 1985, my parents went on a trip to Medjugorje after reading an article about it in *Reader's Digest*. My mother had missed out on her dream of meeting Padre Pio because she was busy raising seven children. When she read about Medjugorje, she did not want to miss this opportunity before it ended. My father was reluctant to travel to a communist country, but my mother was determined and convinced him to go with her. Both of my parents had a tremendous spiritual awakening there and came back on fire. My mother's joyful excitement was inspiring, but what really sparked my interest was the response of my father. A calm, mild-mannered man, I don't recollect my dad ever being as moved or excited about anything, either in magnitude or duration. It was both of my parents' unique reactions that convinced me that something was happening in Medjugorje. They spoke about the Catholic faith with previously unheard passion and they wanted to pray the Rosary together as a family. After sharing their experience, giving us books about the apparitions, and showing us some Medjugorje videos, they made the extraordinary offer of sending all seven children, four of whom had spouses, on a pilgrimage there.

My older brother, Mike, and his wife, Cindy, were the first to take my parents up on their offer and they also had a deep experience of God's presence in Medjugorje. My brother is quiet about personal matters, including his faith. When he and Cindy returned, Mike did not say very much to me, but he took his practice of faith much more seriously, including going to Mass regularly and praying the Rosary. The witness of my parents and my brother (and the fact that the trip would be paid for) led me to go on my first pilgrimage to Medjugorje with my sisters, Mary and Pat, in late June of 1986. My sisters and I had never been to Europe before and we were excited at the prospect of going to another country and possibly experiencing something supernatural.

We traveled with a group of wonderful people and set out to experience everything that was offered in Medjugorje. Each night, as our group gathered for dinner, people would share stories of the incredible things they had witnessed. I yearned to experience these things, but by the third day I realized that I had the wrong frame of mind. I needed to put aside my own superficial desires to be a spectator of miraculous things and really begin to pray and open my heart to God. That's the day I decided to go to Confession, and it proved to be a significant turning point for me. Not only were my sins forgiven, but I also received the grace to move forward in my spiritual life. Interestingly, from that day on, I could see the sun in the miraculous way others had described, with a Eucharist-like disk in front of it, but this miracle seemed to pale in comparison to what was happening to me internally. For the first time, I began to feel the presence of God in my life and in the Eucharist. The Holy Spirit further graced me with a hunger for knowledge about my faith, which was being fed through the homilies of the Franciscans and the books on Catholicism that I began to read there.

I refer to my first trip to Medjugorje as "The Light Show" because in addition to the miracle of the sun, I witnessed two other phenomena. One afternoon, my sister Pat and I went up to Apparition Hill to pray the Rosary together, using instructional booklets to help us since we were new to this prayer. As we gazed over the valley toward St. James Church that summer afternoon, we looked at the sun effortlessly with the protective disk in front of it. A display of God's poetry and power then occurred that will remain with me the rest of my life. Against the backdrop of a clear blue sky, a definitive ring of color formed around the sun, slowly changing hues of red, purple, green, yellow, and dark blue. The solid ring of color had a width approximately the diameter of the sun. Each ring of color lasted a few precious seconds before fading away, leaving only the blue sky. It was one of the most beautiful sights I'd ever seen. This vision was both incredible and peaceful at the same time. Needless to say, we both felt affirmed and encouraged in our attempt to pray the Rosary.

I was also treated to an amazing luminary display in the night sky as I rode in a cab with a fellow pilgrim. We were headed toward Apparition Hill to join our group and others who had been invited to pray with the visionary Ivan and his prayer group. As our cab approached St. James Church with Mt. Krizevac in the background, both of us began to see what looked like fireballs shooting out of the top of the mountain toward Apparition Hill. This was not fireworks, but substantial balls of fire. When we excitedly pointed it out to our driver, he acknowledged it rather calmly. I learned later that cab drivers in those early days often saw remarkable displays like this because they spent so much time outdoors.

When we reached Apparition Hill and stumbled our way up the rocky mountain path in the dark to meet the others, we were surprised to find several thousand people gathered around Ivan and his prayer group. People from all over the world were singing and praying, their voices blending together in a multitude of languages in an angelic manner. It was really very moving. By listening for the English language, we were able to locate our group who confirmed that they, too, had seen the balls of fire in the sky. Praying together that night was an unforgettable experience that furthered my spiritual awakening and solidified my faith.

On the flight home, I was in a state of spiritual shock as I contemplated all that had happened during my pilgrimage. I believed that our Blessed Mother was appearing in Medjugorje and that God truly did exist and, in fact, was active in the world in an imminent way. I quickly realized that my life was pointed completely in the wrong direction. While it was over-

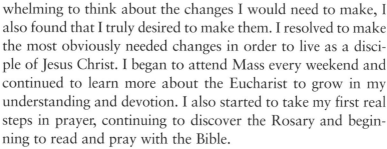

whelming to think about the changes I would need to make, I also found that I truly desired to make them. I resolved to make the most obviously needed changes in order to live as a disciple of Jesus Christ. I began to attend Mass every weekend and continued to learn more about the Eucharist to grow in my understanding and devotion. I also started to take my first real steps in prayer, continuing to discover the Rosary and beginning to read and pray with the Bible.

I arrived home with the desire to share my experience with everyone I knew, but I soon found this to be difficult. My understanding of the Catholic faith was still far from deep and my experience seemed beyond my friends' appreciation, especially my roommate, who was a fallen-away Amish. Perhaps my actions spoke louder than my words, however. Along with other influences, years later, my roommate would become a baptized Christian.

In terms of my career, the shallow dream of becoming a millionaire fell away pretty quickly, but I still had to make a living. I continued my work as a CPA and in my free hours entered into two more real estate projects. My partner was a good practicing Catholic who helped pursue real estate investment in an ethical, Christian manner. I continued to socialize with my CPA friends and began to talk about my faith. It surprised me to learn that many of my friends were practicing Catholics. We had worked together and partied together, but we had not spoken much about our common faith.

The people I found most receptive to my conversion story were those who had also visited Medjugorje. I met many of them when my family and I began to attend annual Medjugorje conferences held at the University of Notre Dame. The conferences were positive experiences that taught me a great deal about the faith. Sister Briege McKenna, O.S.C., was a particularly inspiring speaker with practical advice for faith formation. In one of her talks she stated that we should be signposts for God, pointing people to the Lord through the example of our lives. This thought made complete sense to me. A signpost does not draw people to itself, but points them on the way to their destination. I began to pray daily that I could be a signpost for the Lord, realizing that this would require me to change and grow in my faith. It was then that I felt the desire to begin living more explicitly as a Christian disciple, becoming a eucharistic minister and volunteering to cook at a local soup kitchen. By 1990, I was attending Mass a few days during the week and developing a deep love and appreciation for the Eucharist. Soon even my desire to make a living in real estate investment waned and I informed my business partner that I was no longer interested in making money; instead, I wanted to use my skills and abilities to help people.

In March that year, my parents were returning to Medjugorje. Initially, I declined their invitation to go on the trip thinking that I was "already converted." However, I did have vacation time coming up. My growing social consciousness was challenging me not to spend money wastefully on extravagant purchases and fancy vacations. But when other family members made plans to go, I decided to join them as a guide since I had already been there.

When we arrived in Medjugorje it was pouring rain. The group was disappointed until we learned that the villagers were ecstatic because this marked the end of a potentially crop-damaging drought. The wet weather cancelled some planned group activities and I began to get cabin fever. No longer able to stand it, I started climbing the mountains in the rain. This time alone in prayer ended up being very beneficial to me. It helped me prepare for Confession; however, this time when I received this sacrament, something didn't feel quite right. I felt as if there was some unfinished business to attend to.

My mother had heard that Father Phillip Pavich, O.F.M., was an excellent confessor. The next day I stood on line outside his confessional but I was unable to get in. The following day I went again, arriving early enough to be the second person in line. Father Pavich spent a long time speaking to me, as was his custom with pilgrims, and the experience was extraordinary. He compassionately spoke about every commandment as thoroughly as any catechism and educated me about the ways that they are broken, opening my eyes to the various sinful behaviors in my life. It was the most powerful and thorough confession I have ever made. Father Pavich gave me excellent advice, prayed over me, and granted me absolution, and I basked in deep freedom and forgiveness.

I was bubbling with joy as I took the path through the vineyards and tobacco fields toward the place we were staying. As I walked, I talked to God aloud, thanking Him exuberantly for this wonderful experience of His love and mercy, my deepening conversion, and for the freedom I was now enjoying. It was at this time that a very clear question entered my mind from outside of me. *"Do you want to continue along the path you are on?"* I understood this to mean did I want to continue to live in this joy and to follow the path that had led to it. I replied, "Yes!" immediately. Very clearly, the response came: *"Be a priest."* It was unmistakable to me that this was an invitation from God, perhaps the answer to the daily prayer I had offered for several years, asking for His help in being a signpost for Him. It took me all of a millisecond to accept with my whole heart the invitation to pursue the priesthood. It felt like a perfect fit for my life, as if I had discovered my true self.

As I relished in the double joy of the confessional experience and this mystical conversation with God, I decided that I needed to speak with a priest. I wanted to know what I must do next and give time to allow this paradigm shift in my life's plans to sink in before telling anyone. A young priest in our group gave me very sound guidance. He suggested I affirm God's invitation by living for the next several months as a priest would by going to Mass every day, pursuing a dedicated prayer life, and getting involved in ministries in my parish. I would learn later that this was similar to the advice of St. Ignatius of Loyola for discerning a major decision.

I followed the advice over several months and the calling grew stronger as the days passed. To the surprise and delight of my family, I entered the seminary in the fall of 1990 and was ordained a priest for the Archdiocese of Chicago in 1995. I visited Medjugorje while in the seminary and this, too, was a faith-strengthening blessing.

As a new priest, I was assigned to a wonderful parish where I developed friendships with a number of parishioners. I loved my ministry, parish, and being with people. Then, in 2001, I was asked to leave parish life and join the formation faculty at Mundelein Seminary. The transition was difficult for me for various reasons. To make matters worse, in the spring of 2002 I was appointed vocation director for the Archdiocese of Chicago, taking my post at the height of the priest sexual abuse scandal. I now faced recruiting men during a time when the morale of the Catholic faithful and priests alike was at an incredible low.

Between the job change, transition difficulties, and the priest scandal, I was feeling pretty angry with God. It was affecting my prayer life and my approach to the Mass and the sacraments. My spiritual director, a Jesuit who had never been to Medjugorje, suggested I go back there, calling it the "well of my spiritual life." I made plans in 2003 to attend the annual Medjugorje international priest retreat and arrived a week early to give myself some time to rest and achieve some sense of peace.

After several days of trying to turn things over to God in prayer, I still felt poorly rested and emotionally unresolved. One night I couldn't sleep at all, which was particularly annoying because I had planned to rise early in the morning to climb Mt. Krizevac and avoid the summer heat. Frustrated, I got out of bed at 2:00 a.m. and went to climb the mountain, fueled by the anger that was bottled up inside me. As I ascended, I had a very loud conversation with God, in between praying the Stations of the Cross. At each Station, I would attempt to prayerfully meditate and listen for an answer and then, walking to the next Station, the loud conversation would begin again. I yelled at God about being taken from my parish, about the troublesome transition to the seminary, about the priest scandal, and about being over-worked. There were no mystical conversations or outward luminary signs in the sky to indicate that He was listening. However, somewhere around the twelfth or thirteenth Station, all of the frustration, anger, and anxiety suddenly disappeared. A state of contentedness spread through me: it was the peace of Medjugorje that millions have come to know and cherish. I ended up staying on the mountain for several hours until sunrise enjoying this peace, and I was able to attend the retreat feeling completely rejuvenated.

My experiences of Medjugorje will always remain an important part of my priesthood. It was the Blessed Mother who brought me to her Son, and she continues to intercede for me on a regular basis today. When I look back on the most trying times in my priesthood, I see clearly that these were the times that I waned in praying the Rosary. It's not to say that praying the Liturgy of the Hours, celebrating the Mass, receiving the sacrament of Reconciliation, or ministering to others are not vital or life-giving to my spirituality, but I see a tangible difference when days pass by without praying the Rosary. This prayer simply grounds me in Jesus Christ and puts me in a better spiritual place. Medjugorje introduced me to an inner peace and sheer joy I had not experienced before my conversion. It put a deep desire in my heart to know Jesus Christ and it pointed me in the right direction so that, perhaps, through my Christian discipleship and my priesthood, I may point others to Him as well.

Father Joseph Noonan, Illinois

"Dear children! Also today I call you to prayer. In this time of grace, may the cross be a signpost of love and unity for you through which true peace comes. That is why, little children, pray especially at this time that little Jesus, the Creator of peace, may be born in your hearts. Only through prayer will you become my apostles of peace in this world without peace. That is why, pray until prayer becomes a joy for you. Thank you for having responded to my call."

Message of November 25, 1999

Holy Scripture

*"Dear children, today I call
you to read the Bible every day in
your homes and let it be in a visible place
so as always to encourage you to read it and
to pray."*
Message of October 18, 1984

14
In Your Arms

At the prompting of my mother, I was raised in the Episcopal faith and attended church quite regularly. Although I grew up considering myself a Christian, I came to find out as an adult that I wasn't really living the life of one. It would be the prompting of another Mother, in Medjugorje, that would lead me to go beyond myself, beyond my faith, and even beyond my country, persevering to live the Gospel as a member of the Catholic Church.

Before I ever knew anything about Catholicism or Medjugorje, I was working as a salesman for an oil company in Dallas, Texas. In November 1990, I was in New Orleans attending a sales convention. On Saturday evening of that week, I had gone out to Bourbon Street for business meetings and dinner and had returned home to my hotel room, where I soon fell asleep. That night, I had a most extraordinary dream, unlike any I have ever had before. I dreamt that I was driving along on a mountain road when I suddenly lost control of the car and drove off a cliff. The strange part was that the dream had all the sensations of falling over a cliff in a car. As I was going over, I found myself compressed against the windshield in a fetal position. I could look down at the ground racing quickly toward me, and it was terrifying. Right before impact, I cried out, "God, God, I'm yours—take me in your arms!" With that, I woke up, completely soaked with sweat. Needless to say, I was very thankful to be alive and safe in my hotel room.

The following Saturday, I was involved in a real car accident. I was driving my car along a mountain road, with an abyss on one side and the face of a hill on the other. The car began to swerve down the curvy road aiming at the abyss, but I was able to swing it back toward the hill. In an instant, the car rolled over and I ended up ramming into the hill on the left side of the road. The car flipped completely upside down and after the loud sounds of screeching brakes and crunching metal, everything became instantly quiet. When it was over, I found myself in the fetal position against the windshield of the car, exactly as I had dreamed about a week earlier. However, there were two major differences. The first is that I didn't go over the abyss, and the second is that I didn't have enough time to cry out to God. Fortunately, I was not badly hurt, but the experience had a profound effect on me, making me realize how short and fragile life can be.

A few weeks later, I found out that my parish, St. David's Episcopal Church, was hosting two speakers from the Queen of Peace Center in Dallas. At the time I was on the vestry of the church, so I was aware of all the events that took place there, but this would not normally be something that I would attend. For some unexplainable reason, however, I found myself there that evening to listen to the presentation. To my surprise, my mother also showed up. Neither of us knew anything about Medjugorje.

A woman who ran the Center spoke first. She talked about Mary being our heavenly mother and for the first time in my life, it made total sense to me. This was rather newsworthy, because in my Episcopal experience, Mary was a figure that was placed in the nativity scene at Christmas and was then sort of thrown back in the closet for the rest of the year. But I found myself agreeing with what the speaker was saying that night about the Blessed Mother because it reminded me of my own mother. I also put a lot of credence in what this woman was saying because she was a mother of twelve children.

Next, a man got up to speak. He was a lawyer and he had a rather analytical approach to the whole matter. This also made a lot of sense to me, as I tend to be an analytical person myself. He brought reality to the situation of Medjugorje while the woman added the romance. You might say that he spoke to my mind and she spoke to my heart. All I know is that a light was turned on inside of me that night. After the meeting, I went to look at the books the speakers had brought with them, and I grabbed everything I could about Medjugorje. I took it home and read it all.

Shortly after, I learned about a Medjugorje conference that would take place in Wichita, Kansas, a five- or six-hour drive from my home. I recognized several of the speakers' names from the literature I had picked up at my church and I made the conscious decision to drive up there to see what it was all about. It turned out to be a wonderful experience for me. I was surrounded by five thousand Catholics alive in their faith, and that's where my real conversion began. Things started to make sense to me about the Eucharist, about Jesus being our Savior and Mary being our Mother, and about the true and original Church set in motion by Christ. In my quest for God, I must have stood out in the crowd at that conference, because people kept coming up and talking with me. They were very loving and made me feel right at home.

During the conference, I had the grace to meet a priest named Father Svetozar Kraljevic who spoke about a tremendous need in the region surrounding Medjugorje. Rumors of war were starting and the economy was bad. In his tiny village of Konjic, the people had started an expansion project to a church and no one had any money to finish it. They needed to get a roof on the building before the next winter set in. Father Svet invited anyone interested in learning more about the situation to a talk he was giving later. Thinking that they needed someone to swing a hammer or do other physical work, I went to the meeting with about two hundred other people. I quickly realized that the Franciscans needed money, and I felt disappointed that I had none to offer. Leaving the conference that weekend, I realized my life had completely changed. Despite my newfound joy, I still wished I could do something to help Father Svetozar. I felt called to help, but I just didn't know how.

I don't even remember the passing of time on the drive home that night because so many thoughts were in my head, the most pressing being a desire to go to Medjugorje. The moment I walked in my house I received the news that my grandfather had died. Even death, however, was different for me after that conference and I accepted the news rather peacefully. My grandfather had led a good Christian life and I was confident that he was in a good place. Had I learned this news before the conference on the other hand, I would have been devastated. At the funeral, my aunt told me that my grandfather had left me an inheritance of one thousand dollars. I needed $995 to go on a pilgrimage to Medjugorje and at that moment I knew the money was meant for this purpose.

Meanwhile, I consulted with a few associates about ways to raise money to help with the church project over in Yugoslavia. My friends thought I would have a tough time since I wasn't even Catholic and because most people in America didn't even know where Bosnia was at the time. Someone suggested that I speak with Wayne Weible. His book *Medjugorje, The Message* had just come out, and he was difficult to reach. But through God's grace, I was able to meet with him and his suggestion was that I pray about it. I was rather disappointed at this response because I was hoping this man would have all the answers for me, but I did start to pray. Shortly after that meeting, I went to my mailbox and there was a very substantial check from one of the people I had talked to about the church project. I had gone to him for counsel, not for money, so I called him right away. He told me he knew I was doing the right thing and the money was to help me get started. "Get started?" I repeated. "With this, I'm finished." Before he hung up, he also thanked me for telling him about Medjugorje because it had started to change his life as well.

A month later, in 1991, I was graced to go to Medjugorje for the first time. I was quite prepared for this trip, having read all about it and having prayed many novenas. Although I went with a group, I didn't feel I needed a tour guide because of all the research I had done. Medjugorje quickly became a very special place to me, as it still is today. On that first trip I witnessed the miracle of the sun and at the time I thought it was unbelievable. But as I have matured in my faith and in my experiences of Medjugorje, I've come to realize that these kinds of signs and wonders are not what Medjugorje is about at all. Today I've learned to see that every day is a miracle.

During that pilgrimage, I delivered the money personally to Father Svetozar and he showed me the church in Konjic. Although I didn't know it at the time, this marked the beginning of what would become my ministry in humanitarian relief. It was important to me that the man who donated the money received a tax credit for his generous gift, so we handled the donation through St. David's Episcopal Church. Shortly after, when the war broke out and the region's need became more publicized, people started sending money to St. David's to help with the cause. The pastor put me in charge of the funds and I even went on EWTN a few times to talk about our efforts. Pretty soon the budget for the relief fund was larger than the budget for our little church, and because of a growing concern about liability issues due to the war, we set up a nonprofit entity called St. David's Relief Foundation.

It's hard to summarize all that happened to me the first year after my conversion because things moved so quickly and miracles seemed to happen all around me. The best way I can describe it is to say that I was on a real grace ride. I came to discover some time later that on the night of my car accident, Ivan the visionary was in New Orleans at a Medjugorje conference attended by five thousand people. The theme of the conference was to pray for the conversion of sinners. The following year, I was asked to speak at that same conference. I assured the people in the audience that prayer is not a waste of time—I was a living witness to answered prayers. After doing a few more talks in Dallas and New Orleans, I realized that it was time for me to move on. It was time to stop talking about conversion and time to put it into action.

Early on, I had made a commitment to the people of Bosnia-Herzegovina and to God that as long as people supported our efforts, I would continue to serve in the endeavor of humanitarian relief. Coming from the breadbasket of the world, I knew that something could and should be done. My part, I believe, was to help organize people who also wanted to help in this humanitarian project. A year passed, then two, then three. Fifteen years later, we are still involved in helping people in this region. Somewhere along the way, in 1994, I converted to Catholicism because I accepted it as the one true Church and it was right for me. But the work we do through St. David's Relief is multi-denominational and non-partisan. We are people of all different backgrounds working in unity to help those in need.

St. David's Relief has been blessed to have many volunteers throughout the years. We take our direction from the Franciscans and it has been a wonderful relationship from the beginning. As the situation and needs in Bosnia have changed, we have changed along with it. At first I carried supplies over in suitcases by myself. Then I was joined by a group of people with their suitcases. From there we went to driving convoys from England across Europe with trucks and supplies, leaving all of it behind in Bosnia. Eventually we began delivering goods by the shipload. In time I discerned a need for a warehouse delivery facility in Medjugorje as the Franciscans were struggling with distributing the supplies, and we proceeded to set up that operation as well.

Once I had made my first trip to Medjugorje in 1991, I began going to Bosnia about six times a year for the next several years. Not surprisingly, it became difficult for me to manage my humanitarian work and my job in the oil business. A friend of mine pointed out charitably that I wasn't doing justice to either one and that I needed to make a decision. I took a few days to think and pray about it and decided to leave my job so I could focus my efforts on St. David's Relief. I did this up until 1999 when several circumstances prodded me to think about my own personal financial future. Prior to that, I had ignored any secular offer, as I knew it would distract me from my real purpose. But eventually I started a telecommunications business and split my time between that and the relief work. I was able to sell out of my interest in 2002 and move to the city of Split, in Croatia. Now I am doing work full time for St. David's Relief and waiting for the Lord's next direction.

As a small organization, we try and meet the material demands here as best we can. It seems, however, that in recent times we are transitioning into an organization that introduces people to the region by allowing them the opportunity to work here for a week (which is a grace in itself) and then introducing them to Medjugorje during a second week. It's a project we call "summer work camp" and it has been a phenomenal success. I find it has been a real grace and blessing to be able to introduce so many people to Medjugorje because I enjoy watching God go to work on them. I can tell you almost to the day when each person will get "hit" over the head—it's an absolutely wonderful experience to behold.

Medjugorje is a special place that allows its visitors to recognize that every day is a miracle and a blessing. It achieves this in part, I think, because of its isolated location. Most people who pilgrimage to Medjugorje have to travel some distance; it's not an easy place to get to by any means. From the moment you make the decision to go, the journey begins. Once you arrive it's like a fast, because you are cut off from the people and the culture you are accustomed to. Many of us think of fasting as depriving ourselves of food, but fasting can also be depriving yourself of the norm in order to give God time enough to work on you. You make more space for God in this region because there is a void from the norm, and if you are open, God will fill that void. I think that's one of the biggest miracles of Medjugorje: people come and make room and time for God.

Medjugorje has shown me that God exists and that Jesus is reaching out to each and every one of us. I have come to know His incredibly loving Mother who wants nothing but the best for her children—and that means all of us. Through Medjugorje, God, Jesus, and Mary have jumped off the pages of scripture for me. I grew up where we always had a Bible in the house, but quite frankly it had a bit of dust on it. The Bible seemed to me to be full of text, but not reality. I remember thinking that it would have been a lot easier to believe in this stuff if I had actually lived in the time of Jesus. Today, Medjugorje has brought the Bible alive for me—it has brought *Christ* alive for me—in a way I had never known before. Some people can go through life and have an incredible faith without ever experiencing something of the magnitude of Medjugorje. Others need that little kick in the pants, and maybe that's the reason Medjugorje is here, for people like myself who need that extra boost to enhance their belief.

The message of Medjugorje is very personal when you first discover it and when you are first nurtured by it. But it is not meant to be kept under a bushel basket. You're supposed to take what you've learned, apply it to yourself and your family, and then share it with the rest of the world. Some people spread the message through literature, prayer, words, or actions. We are called to do this in different ways, through our different gifts, and each way is important. In my experience, Medjugorje is the most wonderful place to visit and the most difficult to leave. It can actually be a scary experience to leave, because it is like you are literally leaving your Mother's arms. I've seen a lot of tears flow as people depart this place. They have received so much here, but once they leave it is time to give back.

The truth is, once you've been exposed to Medjugorje you are never the same again. My own life changed dramatically when I was involved in an accident fifteen years ago. My involvement with Medjugorje, on the other hand, has been no accident whatsoever.

Jeff Reed, Split, Croatia

"Dear children! In this time of grace again I call you to prayer. Pray little children, for unity of Christians, that all may be one heart. Unity will really be among you inasmuch as you will pray and forgive. Do not forget: love will conquer only if you pray, and your heart will open. Thank you for having responded to my call."

Message of January 25, 2005

15
Long Have I Waited

The desire to become a priest was impressed upon my heart as a young child by the kind and gracious example of several holy priests who blessed me with their presence throughout my Catholic schooling in the Jersey City, New Jersey, area. In particular, I credit Father Ben Piazza, a gentle and loving man of God who celebrated the Mass so beautifully. To me, he was a saint. The Blessed Mother also held a role of importance in my developing spirituality, starting in my two grade schools, Our Lady of Sorrows and Our Lady of Czestochowa. I must have had a great love for the Mother of God as a child, because I can remember a little ritual I used to perform when I was about ten or twelve years old. My family attended St. Dennis Church in Manasquan, New Jersey, which had a beautiful statue of Our Lady in the front yard. After Mass, when I was certain that no one was watching, I would shyly run up to the statue and kiss her feet. Then I would run away.

During my high school years at St. Aloysius—years I cherish fondly—there were two Jesuit priests who had a particular influence on me. Father George Mader introduced me to the good work of helping the poor. I was impressed by his sensitivity to those less fortunate and I accompanied him often to the projects to help him in his endeavors. Father Frank McNulty was another wonderful influence. He was a young, good-looking priest and a hero to his students, kind of like Father O'Malley in *Going My Way*. I never thought Father McNulty took much notice of me so I was quite pleased, therefore, when he told my parents how proud he was of me at graduation. That praise reinforced my desire to serve God all the more.

After high school, I attended St. Peter's College, where I studied history and played sports. But always in the back of my mind I knew what I wanted to do when I graduated: I wanted to be a priest. Because of my respect for the Jesuit high school teachers, I applied to their seminary first, but I was not accepted. It may have been that my grades did not quite meet their demanding academic standards, or it may have been attributed to health issues. I had been diagnosed with a persistent ulcer at the age of sixteen, caused, I'm sure, by growing up in a Polish/Irish home where I learned to hold my emotions inside. I applied then to the diocese and was accepted with the prerequisite that I spend one year at Seton Hall University to study Latin and Greek, which I enjoyed very much.

My five years at Immaculate Conception Seminary in the archdiocese of Newark was like a piece of heaven for me. The seminary was packed with over three hundred energetic young men, confirming that this was a wonderful path I had chosen. I loved the religious garb we wore, I enjoyed my classes, and I participated in all kinds of sports and recreations. Seminary was like my Camelot. Each year we volunteered for summer assignments and I always chose work in the inner city because I enjoyed working with the poor. I worked in the same projects I had visited with Father Mader and found it to be both rewarding and affirming. Only two things darkened my happiness during the early years of seminary: my stomach ulcer, which warranted surgery, and the death of my father in the

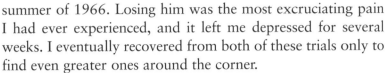

summer of 1966. Losing him was the most excruciating pain I had ever experienced, and it left me depressed for several weeks. I eventually recovered from both of these trials only to find even greater ones around the corner.

In 1968, Pope Paul VI released the controversial encyclical *Humanae Vitae,* and with that, a spirit of rebellion began to enter the seminary. Not all of the professors were on the same page about the document's tough stance against birth control. In class, we were receiving two theories. Some of the professors taught that people could practice artificial contraception if they thoroughly examined their consciences and believed it was all right. It was the Holy Father's dictate and the teaching of the Church, but you could go against it. This confused and hurt me. I felt as though the strong foundation I had been standing on was beginning to soften. Laxity was setting in. Two of my professors actually left the priesthood and I was scandalized. My ideals and my image of the priesthood were deeply wounded.

There was another controversy brewing, this one having to do with celibacy. Several priests felt that the Church's teaching on this subject was outdated and that change was around the corner. I was particularly vulnerable in the area of celibacy because physical attention was not a strong and healthy part of my childhood. I struggled with an unmet need deep inside me, of which the devil soon began to take advantage. For a while I didn't know if I would make it to ordination and I held myself up for the orders of subdiaconate because of my insecurities. The following year, however, I petitioned and received it and I was ordained a priest in 1970. I remember crying continuously during the entire liturgy. Some of the tears came from the joy of finally achieving my childhood dream, but some of them reflected the sadness of knowing that my image of the priesthood was no longer the same.

Things did not improve much after ordination. My first assignment, at a parish in Elizabeth, New Jersey, was neither a holy nor prayerful environment for me. An unhealthy spirit had taken over and I was scandalized by what I thought was an immoral act in the rectory, but I didn't have the courage to bring it up. In addition, the priests were not involved with the poor, which I still held as a high priority. To buffer myself from the evil around me, I immersed myself in work by going out to the worst sections of the city and bringing children back to play in the school gym. I decided these children needed special programs for academics and recreation, which I began to coordinate with great zeal.

The parishioners complained that I wasn't spending enough time with the children of the parish and I began to be ostracized. I loved the parish children; I just couldn't abandon these less fortunate individuals. Some of the inner city children seemed beyond help because of their deep wounds, so I decided to take some child psychology classes at Fordham University in New York. This is when I made my first big mistake: I believed the answer to my situation was in science and not in Jesus Christ. Because I was so busy running programs and studying, I stopped praying the breviary. I just didn't have the time to pray and meditate on the Word of God. I was full of myself, quite rebellious, running my programs the way I wanted to despite how people around me felt. The more I worked with the youth, the more isolated I became from the priests.

I needed help with my programs, so I solicited students from high school and the university. In no time, I found myself surrounded by young, attractive women, a few of whom had left their convents. A transition was happening in me: I was becoming more secularized and, at the same time, weaker and more vulnerable. It began innocently enough by working on school projects together with young women and it progressed to going out to dinner with some of them. Things were getting more and more confusing. Finally, I called a trusted monsignor I knew from seminary and told him if I didn't get help I was going to leave the priesthood. He sent me to see a priest psychologist in New York, but I felt he was crazier than I was. My whole world was turning upside down.

When things looked like they couldn't get any worse, they did. I put myself in harm's way one too many times with women. I was at the rectory feeling lonely one night so I called one of the young girls who helped with my programs and she invited me over. That night, I fell into sin. It left me feeling completely crushed and destroyed, as if all the life had been pulled out of me. I was like a dead man walking. That weekend, I left the rectory and never said Mass again.

After fifteen months in the priesthood, I had walked away from my dream. I needed some consolation, and I found it in the company of a beautiful young woman named Kathy who had worked with me in my social programs. She had left her religious vocation as well and we began dating. Three months later we were engaged and I applied for laicization. Deep down, however, I did not really want to leave the priesthood, but my pride prevented me from going to Confession and being honest with Kathy and myself. I made my own criteria for judgment and no longer believed in the mercy of God. Kathy and I decided not to wait for the laicization process to be completed. The following year we married in an Episcopal church. As I was walking down the aisle, I heard a voice in my ear saying, *"You are doing the wrong thing.*" I remember thinking back, "Leave me alone. You didn't make me happy." I was willful and completely self-absorbed.

Not surprisingly, our marriage was fraught with problems. I was attracted to Kathy and I loved her very much, but something was always missing. I started studying pre-med and working in a hospital as if becoming a doctor would make it up to the Lord for leaving the priesthood. Kathy hated my long hours and heavy class load. I switched over to education and got a teaching certificate so I could begin working with poor children, which at least fulfilled my desire for ministry. This job, however, was also detrimental to our marriage, because I once again immersed myself in after-school programs. When we had two daughters together, I buried the idea of ever returning to the priesthood. And with that, I also buried my hope for complete happiness.

After thirteen years, Kathy and I separated. The papers had come in from Rome about my laicization, but I had no desire to sign them. I was so selfish, I wanted Kathy *and* the priesthood. It was like I was living in this dichotomized world. Three years later, Kathy and I were divorced. The guilt of having failed for a second time and the thought of my children having to grow up in a broken home drove me back to prayer in order to save the marriage. I needed a miracle. That's when I learned about Medjugorje, and in November 1990 I decided to go there to seek a miracle for family healing.

My trip was blessed from the beginning when I was providentially seated next to a man named Charlie Gibbons on the flight over. Charlie was an international tax accountant lawyer who made good money. For eight hours, he told me story after story about the miracles people experienced in Medjugorje. He was making this particular pilgrimage to thank the Blessed Mother for a miracle involving his two-year-old son who had a condition in which his brain was falling out of his skull. Although he was not a churchgoer at the time, Charlie prayed to the Blessed Mother and said, "Please just cradle my son in your arms." After surgery, a female neurologist walked up to Charlie and said, "I don't know how to explain this, but your son came out of a very difficult surgical procedure extremely well, almost as if someone were holding him in his arms and loving him." By the time our plane landed, I had fallen in love with Medjugorje and I was hopeful that I, too, might experience a miracle.

On the second day of our pilgrimage, we went to hear Father Jozo Zovko speak. Charlie had told me some pretty amazing stories involving this priest, so I felt a great deal of awe and respect for him. Father Jozo, through his interpreter, Anka, started to talk about the priesthood. As he spoke, I felt myself slowly sliding out of the pew into a kneeling position on the hard marble floor and tears began to flow. He spoke for two hours, talking about how the devil targets priests, how he gets them to fall, and why it is so important to pray for these men. By this point, I was crying like a baby. But I was also quite confused. I hadn't come to Medjugorje to return to the priesthood; I had come for a family healing. Why wasn't Jesus listening? After Father Jozo's talk, I jotted him a note and left it with one of the assistants. I told him that I had left the priesthood twenty years ago and asked if I could talk to him about it.

On the last night of our pilgrimage, the phone rang at ten o'clock. It was Anka calling, asking me when I could see Father Jozo. I told her I was leaving first thing in the morning, so she invited me to see him that night. On the long cab ride to Tihaljina, I began to regret ever writing that note. I didn't really want to tell Father Jozo all of my sins. But when we arrived at one o'clock in the morning, I was surprised to see the gentle priest standing outside the rectory waiting for me. That impressed me very much. He put his arms around me and greeted me warmly with one word, *"Father."* I had not been addressed by that name for twenty years. We went inside and through the help of Anka's interpretation, I told him everything that had happened to me, from my childhood desires to be a priest, to the scandals in the rectory, how I had fallen and never said Mass again. Father Jozo listened to my story and then stood up. He said only two lines. "You are to go back in [to the priesthood] for your wife's soul and the souls of your children. You are the greatest thing to happen in Medjugorje in years because you are a priest returning, from which many others will follow." He also encouraged me to return to Medjugorje with my family.

On the way home, I felt so free and alive; there was a joy in me I hadn't experienced for twenty years. It was the joy I had lost when I fell into sin, and now it was given back to me. I was determined to return to the priesthood, a long and difficult journey that would take thirteen years—one for every year that I had been married. But now I had the enthusiasm to accomplish it.

My first thought was to pursue the idea of remarrying in the Eastern Rite so that I could save my family *and* my priesthood. I was still trying to do things my way. This idea was not even presented to Kathy, however, since she flatly refused my invitation to return to Medjugorje with me. She was convinced I had lost my mind. Kathy's rejection and my distance from Medjugorje began to weaken me again, and I started questioning what a Croatian priest could possibly know about my destiny. Finally, I decided that I needed to speak with an American priest. That very day, I received a postcard from Anka with a picture of the Blessed Mother on it. She wrote, "Be strong in faith and gentle in love as Mary. P. S. Telephone Father Tim Deeter at St. Helen's Church in Orangefield, Texas." Excitedly, I contacted Father Tim and he advised me to do whatever Father Jozo suggested as long as it was within the parameters of the Church. He explained that he had made a trip to Medjugorje incognito to check it out. He was sitting outside St. James Church and as Father Jozo preached the homily in Croatian, Father Tim was able to understand every word. This story convinced me that the Holy Spirit was working through this Croatian priest and I eagerly signed up for another pilgrimage.

My second trip to Medjugorje was a blessing as well, but there were no big pronouncements from Father Jozo. I began to think I had made a mistake in returning. It was painful to have my hopes raised like this. On the last day of my pilgrimage I was anxious to go home and vowed never to return to Medjugorje again. As I was waiting for the bus, a little French priest came to St. James to say Mass. I had already attended Mass that morning, but I had time to kill, so I followed him in. When the priest began his homily to the small group of people in the chapel, he looked directly at me. He said, "Do not ever judge a priest. A man can go back twenty years in time." I couldn't believe what he was saying. "The devil targets a priest," the French cleric continued. "If he gets a priest to fall, many are lost." I began to cry. This man seemed to know all my sins. After Mass, I asked him how he knew. He told me he just knew. When I asked him what I should do, he simply answered, "Pray."

On the way home, I was once again on fire. Now I was sure that Our Lord and Our Lady were serious: they really wanted me to come back to the priesthood. My faith was fully restored. I could have flown back to the states without an airplane, I was so happy. I wanted to return to Medjugorje to figure out how this would be accomplished, so this time I arranged to go for a summer. During my third trip, I received many confirmations. Father Jozo counseled me, telling me not to worry, that God would help me. One day, as I was leaving St. James, a woman in the church said to me, "When you sat in front of me today, there was a song that came into my mind: 'Long have I waited for your coming home to me.'" Her words took me off-guard and made me cry, because that song, "Hosea," was the only song I used to sing to Kathy in our early years of marriage. No one would have known that little bit of intimacy but Jesus Christ Himself.

Perhaps the most striking confirmation that summer came from a sixty-seven-year-old Australian Redemptorist priest who had the gift of healing and speaking in tongues. He knew many things about my past just by looking at me, which convinced me that he was genuine. In one conversation, he was speaking in tongues and translating for me. He told me that in five years I would be well on my way to where Our Lady wanted me to be. In seven more years, I would come back to say thank you. He spoke in tongues once more and said, "The word Capuchin comes to mind." At that moment, I decided I had enough confirmation that Our Lady was behind all of this and I returned home to take concrete steps to reclaim my vocation.

The archbishop of Newark was very kind and listened to my story with compassion. He wanted to test if this was indeed the work of the Holy Spirit and told me I would have to wait seven years until my youngest child reached the age of eighteen before we could initiate paperwork. In the meantime, I wrote to the Holy Father about my situation and he responded that he would pray for my intentions. I also returned to Medjugorje often, where Our Lady gave me encouragement.

I credit Our Lady for restoring my faith and making me fall in love again with the Church as my mother. But there were two other sources of grace that helped me on my long journey back to priesthood. The first was the counsel of Father Benedict Groeschel. I was told that he was an excellent priest and psychologist who had helped other priests return to their vocations, *and* he was a Capuchin. This was the deciding factor for me to contact him and my meetings with him proved to be most beneficial.

I also discovered wisdom and truth through the NeoCatechumenate. The twelve-year walk I made (and continue to make) with this movement has helped me to understand my past and change my future. I realized that I had suffered because of my sins and my selfishness; I had been disobedient and arrogant and I needed to face that. I also came to appreciate celibacy as a miracle of grace because it is an outward sign that Jesus Christ can fulfill a person. It became clear to me that when I stopped saying the breviary, I had done more than close a book. I had closed the door to life, and that's why I fell. Now, I was reading and praying these beautiful verses of scripture again, not as an obligation, but out of true love for Jesus, and the Word of God was healing to my soul.

Despite my spiritual conversion, Rome did not make it easy for me to come back to the priesthood after my long absence. They required me to return to the seminary for a year to refurbish my theology. I had to live in a parish as an active member, continue to meet monthly with Father

Groeschel for counseling, and do public hours of reparation. I also had to take a battery of psychological and intelligence tests. Although I met all of these requirements, none of the bishops I approached at first would accept me. I began to doubt for the first time since my summer in Medjugorje that I would ever return to the priesthood. Discouraged, I wrote to the Holy Father again, who responded to me on June 25, the anniversary of the apparitions of Medjugorje, "I will pray that you will receive the sustaining grace of Jesus Christ." It was this sustaining grace that saw me through five additional years until I finally received my priestly faculties back in June of 2003.

The following June, I returned to Medjugorje to thank Our Lady for bringing me back to the priesthood. I was able to concelebrate Mass on the main altar of St. James, a tremendous honor and blessing for me. To my great surprise and delight, the entrance song for the Mass that day was "Hosea." At the words "Long have I waited for your coming home to me," a tear rolled down my cheek. I was home.

Father Robert Sadleck, New Jersey

"Dear children, I, your Mother, love you and wish to urge you to prayer. I am tireless, dear children, and I am calling you even then, when you are far away from my heart. I am a Mother, and even though I feel pain for each one who goes astray, I forgive easily and am happy for every child who returns to me. Thank you for having responded to my call."
Message of November 14, 1985

16
Two Hearts

Our Mother has a way of drawing each of her children into her heart, and for me it was through the example and witness of my own earthly mother. The messages of Medjugorje began to have an effect on my life in the mid- to late-1980s, when my mother began to read and live the messages. She had a book called *Medjugorje, Day by Day* by Father Richard Beyer that had a message, scripture passage, meditation, and application for each day of the year. This little book was instrumental in helping us to incorporate the messages into our daily lives.

I was just a child of nine or ten back then, so it was a fairly simple process for me to watch my mother live the messages and then try to follow in her steps. As I watched my mother pray the Rosary or saw her reading from the Bible or her Medjugorje book, I would ask her what she was doing. She would always stop and teach me, letting me read from her book or pray with her. Her gentle approach never made me feel forced or pressured. This positive childhood experience allowed God to draw me through a grace-filled desire to imitate my mother; and then, so peacefully and naturally, it became a yearning to imitate Our Heavenly Mother and fulfill her every wish.

Total consecration to Our Lady was the next step for my mother in her deepening spirituality. As with the Rosary and the messages, when I saw my mother preparing for the total consecration through the method of St. Louis de Montfort, I too, desired to follow. At the time I didn't know exactly what I was doing, but Our Heavenly Mother did. Not surprisingly, after the consecration, I became drawn to Our Lord's presence in the Eucharist, as Our Lady always leads us to her Son. I began making visits after school to a local parish, where I would meet Jesus in the silence of the little church and long to be with Him, falling more in love with each passing day. I also started joining my parents for Mass on Wednesday mornings before school. Both of my parents are daily communicants, and it gives me particular pleasure to know that even as a baby in my mother's womb, I was graced to be nourished by our sweet Jesus.

Perhaps the only part of my mother's spiritual practices that was difficult for me initially was the discipline of fasting. When I first saw my mother restricting herself to bread and water for Our Lady's intentions, I thought there was no way I could ever do that. But little by little, step by step, Our Lady taught me. First it was one meal of bread only, then two, then a whole day, then two days. By the end of my junior or senior year in high school, I was fasting every Wednesday and Friday in response to Our Lady's request.

With the seed of the messages planted firmly in my heart, I went away to study theology and philosophy at the Franciscan University of Steubenville (FUS) in Ohio. There my soul was awakened to the joys of fellowship with others who were excited about living their faith. Through my classes, the example of my wonderful professors, and the daily spiritual life on campus, I learned the beauty and splendor of the Catholic Church and all of her teachings. Everything that had been planted in my heart while I was at home began to take deeper root. Mass, the Rosary, and Holy

Hours became daily practices, which nourished my spirit. I began reaching out to others through the University Works of Mercy ministry and Life in the Spirit seminars. The environment of faith at Steubenville was rich with constant opportunities to grow and embrace, with all the enthusiasm that comes with youth, the challenges of living an authentic Catholic life.

It was during college that I became aware of the first stirrings of a calling to a religious vocation. This, too, was a step-by-step process, as first a seed must be planted, then watered, then exposed to the sun to blossom fully. I had attended public school from elementary grades through high school and my only contact with religious sisters was in preschool. The idea of becoming a sister never crossed my mind. In fact, when my friends learned of the college I had chosen and the course of study, they teased me, telling me I was going to become a nun. I assured them that I was not going to become a nun.

Our plans, however, are not always the Lord's, and thankfully, I had made that total consecration as a child. While I may have forgotten about it, Our Lady did not, and she was with me in college to guide me. There I renewed the thirty-three-day preparation for Total Consecration to Jesus through Mary. On the day I renewed the consecration, I heard the sweet voice of my Beloved calling. Over the next four years, as my relationship with Jesus and Mary matured, the call became clearer. My response to that call, by the grace of God, also became more and more steadfast.

I began taking steps toward a life of consecration, first by deciding not to date for a semester. When that produced fruits of peace and joy, I continued on that path and took the next step of meeting with other young women who were discerning their vocations. The call seemed most clear to me when my heart was still and silent. To achieve that peace, I spent a semester at the FUS campus in Gaming, Austria. The campus is considerably smaller than Steubenville and there are fewer distractions there. Everyone went to the same Mass, the same classes, the same little dining hall, and every night there was a Holy Hour. On weekends you could travel through Europe and walk where the saints had walked and pray where they had prayed. I wasn't actively discerning my vocation, but in the silence God spoke, and every day it became clearer until I could no longer deny it.

The next step was to find out exactly where God was calling me. A professor at the university, Dr. Mark Miravalle, told a friend of mine about a new religious community that was just being formed. Dr. Miravalle was my teacher and theology thesis advisor. I went to him to inquire about this new order and as he told me about it he would say, "Pray about it; if you feel peaceful, come back and I'll tell you more." Well, I prayed about it and felt great peace, so I kept coming back for more. I discovered that this new order was a eucharistic and contemplative community consecrated to the hearts of Jesus and Mary. There was a house and property in Hopedale, Ohio, but no one was living there yet. The community would consist of priests, brothers, sisters, and lay members. Everything about it sounded appealing.

When I was finally able to see the daily schedule and read the constitution for the Order, my heart leapt and cried out, "This is me! This is everything that Our Lady has been forming me to be!" All the prayers were to be prayed before Jesus exposed in the Blessed Sacrament. The full Rosary and Divine Chaplet were to be prayed daily. There were two Holy Hours in the afternoon and a third one in the evening.

The schedule also included corporal works of mercy, Stations of the Cross on Fridays, and fasting on Wednesdays and Fridays, just like Our Lady asked in Medjugorje. All this was done for the love of the Two Hearts, in reparation for sins committed against them and for souls.

As I considered the challenges of being on the ground floor of a new community, Our Lady once again used my earthly mother to encourage me. She told me, "Monica, sometimes we have to take risks for Jesus." Therefore, with the support of my parents, the guidance of Our Lady, and the burning desire to belong totally to Jesus, that September of 1998 I joined the Order of the Sacred and Immaculate Hearts of Jesus and Mary. I became a postulant on October 13 and was graced with an understanding that this is what I had been created for; this was the answer to the call; this is where I was to become a saint and live all that Our Mother had taught me. Now, the little seed that had taken root could begin to sprout.

When I first joined the order, I was the only one who had not actually been to Medjugorje, but all of us were profoundly affected by and committed to living the messages. It was a joy for me to see how many people Our Lady had drawn into deeper union with her Son, and our common bond made my early years of formation an exciting time filled with many graces. In March of 1999 I became Sister Teresa of the Two Hearts, with Mother Teresa of Calcutta as my patroness. Today I am joined in community by another sister, two brothers, a Benedictine priest who is our Superior, and eight external members, including Dr. Miravalle and his wife.

I feel so blessed to be a part of this special community. The joys, challenges, graces, and trials have all been abundant and I thank God for each of them. Here at the Order, I believe that we are living the messages of Our Lady in Medjugorje: prayer from the heart, fasting, scripture reading, Eucharist, and consecration to the Two Hearts. A few months after my final profession, as a special celebration, my mother brought me to Medjugorje. We were there during the feasts of the Hearts of Jesus and Mary and the whole trip was like a huge hug from Our Lady. Everything I loved about Medjugorje was exactly what I loved about being a member of the Order: the Masses, praying the Rosary before Mass and throughout the day, the Holy Hours, Stations of the Cross, and fasting. On the first day we were there, the priest at St. James Church spoke about entering into the Mass by offering with the gifts that are brought up to the altar either a wound that needs healing or a gift for which we are grateful. I gave to God the gift He has given to me: my vocation. The whole pilgrimage became a thanksgiving from my heart to God and Our Lady, and a confirmation from their hearts to mine that I am blooming where I have been planted. It was only fitting that I was in Medjugorje with my mother, who started it all by her good example, to celebrate the vocation and the Order to which the messages have led. Truly, Our Mother has done great things for me, and holy is her name!

Sister Teresa of the Two Hearts, Ohio

"Dear children! Also today, I urge you to consecrate yourselves to my heart and to the heart of my Son Jesus. Only in this way will you be mine more each day and you will inspire each other all the more to holiness. In this way joy will rule your hearts and you will be carriers of peace and love. Thank you for having responded to my call."

Message of May 25, 2004

17
Coins for the Master

My father came from a family of English descent with a lineage that could be traced back to the pilgrims on the Mayflower. Although the pilgrims left England to escape ongoing religious persecution, there was no outward religious fervor on my dad's side of the family. My grandparents on my mother's side came from Saint Michael's in the Azores, a group of small islands off the coast of Portugal. They came across the ocean with ten children when my mother was just a little girl. The ship arrived at Ellis Island, New York. After immigration processing, they settled in Taunton, Massachusetts, a town highly populated by a Portuguese community devoted to the Fatima apparitions of 1917, but their strong spirituality had no effect on my family. None of us attended church, and other than a "Now I lay me down to sleep" prayer taught to me by my mother, I grew up for the most part ignorant about God.

In January 1984, I turned on the television and found myself watching a documentary narrated by actor Orson Wells on the prophecies of Nostradamus. I had never heard of Nostradamus before nor was I the kind of person to believe in prophecy hogwash by religious fanatics. I had lived long enough to know that life is full of sorrow and suffering. I believed that if there was a God there would be none of this; a real God would be able to keep things in order, protecting us from disease, pain, and evil. Simply put, I was an atheist who was convinced that God was created for people who were afraid of death. I made a decision after watching that ridiculous program to spend the next several months proving that God and Satan did not exist. From January to May, I spent as many hours as I could sitting at the kitchen table with a Bible, references, maps, and other materials. I was determined to find every contradiction I could in scripture, and nothing could deter me.

By May, however, I was not feeling quite myself so I made an appointment to visit my doctor. After describing my symptoms to him, he decided to perform an electrocardiogram (EKG). I lay there patiently watching him look at the results, his face clearly showing that something was not right. He decided to run another EKG before informing me that I had had a myocardial infarction, or a heart attack. In my case this meant that the lower left lobe of my heart was no longer functional and there was a blockage leading from the left to the right side of the heart. Normally, when a person has a heart attack he experiences chest tightness and pain down the arm. What I had is called a silent heart attack and, at age thirty-four, I was shocked and angry and afraid. I was placed on a number of different heart medications and spent a great deal of time at the doctor's office over the following weeks having regular EKG testing.

Eventually the doctor told me that I needed a pacemaker. The thought of being cut open was very disconcerting to me. For weeks I moped around the yard feeling sorry for myself. Every little pain that came my way made me fear it was the beginning of the "big one." The night before I was to meet with the surgeon and discuss the procedure, I recalled passages in the Bible about Jesus healing people during His ministry. Suddenly, because of my predicament, this information was noteworthy. After thinking about it for a while, I decided to entreat God to heal me; I was that desperate. Feeling I had nothing to lose but my pride, this self-proclaimed atheist got on his knees and prayed. I mustered up enough courage to talk to thin air and said, "Okay Jesus, this is Your chance to prove Yourself to me. If You went around healing all these people as the Bible says, then show me You are for real: heal me and I will believe." No sooner did I say this than I felt a tingling in my toes, much like the sensation of a foot falling asleep. The tingling slowly worked its way up through my body and then suddenly rushed through me. I felt as if someone had removed the top portion of my head and a stream of poison was flowing out of me. Then, at once, it was over and I had an immediate feeling of peace and well-being.

When I arrived at the surgeon's office the next day, I interrupted his routine explanation of the pacemaker procedure to happily inform him that it wasn't necessary after all; Jesus had healed me. The heart surgeon told me politely that in times like these it is normal to seek comfort in faith, but the medical reports showed every indication of my need for a pacemaker. I insisted about my healing until finally the doctor agreed to give me another EKG, which came out normal. Ignoring my smile, he ordered a dye test that took seven days. It, too, showed no signs of myocardial infarction or any blockage, for that matter. In fact, the test determined there was no build-up of harmful cholesterol, which the report said was quite remarkable for a man my age. Not only was I healed, Jesus also saw to it that my arteries were flowing with good, clean blood. This was more then I had asked for in my prayers.

After this miracle, I was a new person. I spent every free moment with my nose stuck in the Bible. This time however,

I was not trying to prove that God didn't exist; I was now trying to learn everything I could about Him. I can't begin to count the hours, days, months, and years I spent in pursuit of God. It was nothing for me to watch the sunlight shining in the window after having spent the entire night searching the scriptures. I had promised God that if He healed me I would believe, and I was good to my word. I filled notebook after notebook with discoveries I made in scripture until I decided to invest in a computer. In an effort to devour every bit of information about God—and perhaps to improve my typing skills—I decided to type the entire New Testament, not once, but twice. I'm sure some of my friends thought I had gone quite mad. Their steadfast atheist friend had made a conversion the likes of Ebeneezer Scrooge's.

In late spring of 1989, I was sharing my testimony with a Catholic woman who responded by handing me an envelope of newspaper clippings about a place where apparitions of the Virgin Mary were supposedly taking place. I thanked her for the information but I had no intention of reading it. I put the envelope on the bottom shelf of my coffee table and thought no more about it. A few weeks later during prayer I heard an inner voice say, *"I want you to go to Medjugorje."* I did not even know what *Medjugorje* meant and I tried to ignore this strange voice, but it persisted. I heard it repeatedly over the next few weeks, and often times it woke me in the middle of the night. One evening while talking to my sister on the phone, I told her about the voice I was hearing, because I felt I had to tell someone. When I tried to pronounce the word *Medjugorje* to the best of my ability, I was surprised that my sister had heard of this place. Her pastor, Father Kelly, was taking a group of pilgrims there. I wanted to meet with Father Kelly to learn more about Medjugorje, but was told me that the pastor was a busy man and that he most likely would not be able to see me. As I hung up the phone, I spied the envelope given to me by the Catholic woman a few weeks earlier. I pulled it out and read the word *Medjugorje* on the cover. Inside was information about pilgrimages there. One of them was under the direction of Father Kelly from my sister's parish. Determined, I phoned for an appointment with Father Kelly. Soon after, I met with him and signed up for the September 1989 pilgrimage.

I think that because of my background as an atheist, God wanted to make sure I believed without any shadow of a doubt that Medjugorje is real. Therefore, my pilgrimage was showered with the most extraordinary supernatural experiences from the first day to the last. By the end of the week, the events that happened to me in Medjugorje gave me all the proof I needed—and then some—to know with every fiber of my being that God existed. My experiences were a gift, but they do not mean that I am special in any way. On the contrary, it only shows me what a stubborn person I am. In scripture, Jesus said, "Blessed are they who believe and have not seen." I deeply admire those who believe in God by faith alone, but I was not one of them. I was more like St. Paul, converted by the power of God in an extraordinary way to becoming a Christian with a deep devotion and commitment.

After my return from Medjugorje, my decision to pursue Christianity led me to the Catholic Church, primarily because of the strong love and devotion that I had developed for Our Lady. From that point, my faith grew by leaps and bounds. I was so full of the Spirit that I was constantly immersed in prayer and scripture, and I could not imagine a day going by without attending Mass. Meanwhile, I continued to spread the good news of my healing and began to broach the subject of Medjugorje with strangers, although I kept a low profile around people I knew personally. I didn't want my friends to think I had gone off the deep end. One day, in a local coffee shop, a regular customer remarked, "Michael, what has happened to you? There is a glow about you." This comment took me off guard. Was my joy that evident that people could see it without me saying a word? I went home that morning to look at myself in the mirror and see what the man was talking about. While I could not see a glow on the outside, I was certainly feeling it on the inside. There was a sensation like hunger growing inside of me; I wanted to tell the whole world that God existed, and yet, I was afraid.

My physical healing was one thing; it was a medically proven fact. The miracles I experienced in Medjugorje, however, were different. They were spiritual, supernatural, and very personal, and at first I was reluctant to talk about them with just anyone. In time I realized I could no longer discriminate with whom I shared my stories. I recalled the numerous miracles Jesus performed during His ministry. Some people who received the miracles were told by Jesus to show themselves to the elders so that they would believe. I realized that offering witness and testimony was a wonderful way to thank God for the gifts I had received and a great way to tell the world that Jesus is indeed the Son of God. I also considered the story of the master who gave three coins to one servant, two to another, and a single coin to a third. When the master returned some time later, he called his servants to find out what they had done with the coins he had left in their charges. The servant with three coins had earned another three. The servant with two coins had also doubled his. The servant with one coin, however, had only one to show; he had buried the coin in the ground to keep it safe. The master, disappointed with this third servant's choice, took back the coin, admonished him, and sent him away. When God, the ultimate Master, comes to us and gives us a gift of His choosing, we are not to bury it. We are to do something with it. And what would please the Master more than using our gift to help lost souls?

With new courage, I ventured to tell more people about my healing and about my pilgrimage to Medjugorje. I spoke a few times at church and to a few different social groups as well. From time to time I was invited to homes to talk to small groups. I did the best I could to spread the messages as Our Lady asked, but somehow I felt I was not doing enough. In my prayers I told God that I wanted to do more, but I had to be patient and wait for His plan and His time.

One evening I was looking at the local paper when a flyer for adult education classes fell out of it. As I picked it up, I noticed a class on creating a Web site that piqued my interest and on impulse, I signed up for the class. At the end of the first day, I realized I had a lot to learn about Web site design. The teacher asked us to choose a subject matter for our Web site by the next class. That was something I had not even thought about; what could I possibly have to say to people that would make them want to read what I published on the Internet? Then I thought about Medjugorje and I decided to put up a Web site called, "Miracles and Wonders of Medjugorje." It went online on October 30, 1997, a simple one-page site indicative of my amateur skills. I was committed to this project and in no time, one page turned into twenty. Before long I had so many people visiting my Web site that my Internet service provider started charging me extra money each month for the amount of bandwidth I was using. That's when I decided to move the Web site to a Web hosting company and become a real Web site with a ". org" address. Because "Miracles and Wonders of Medjugorje" was such a long name, I had to change it, and thus "Medjugorje USA" was born.

I had no grand expectations for the Web site; if a few people visited it each week I would have been more than satisfied. God evidently had different plans because, since its original posting, Medjugorje USA has welcomed over twenty-six million visitors! Each week, upwards of forty thousand people browse the site to read Our Lady's messages, conversion stories, news and events, interviews with the visionaries, and more. The Web site has been an immeasurable blessing for me. It is not uncommon to receive e-mails from people who had fallen away from their faith only to have it renewed by the Web site. This has been my greatest reward through the years, and nothing excites me more then knowing that a lost soul has been saved.

I once had a couple write a note of thanks to Medjugorje USA. Their marriage had broken down and they were in the process of divorce, although they were living in the same house until the paperwork was finalized. The woman was surfing the net and found Medjugorje USA by accident. As she was looking at the site, her husband pulled up a chair to see what she was reading. They sat there for hours paging through the information posted there and later they talked about how they had fallen away from their faith. In the beginning of their marriage they had both gone to church, but life circumstances had caused them to drift away. Having read about Medjugorje on my Web site, the couple decided to go to Mass together that Sunday. Their e-mail told me that from there they returned to daily Mass, started praying the Rosary together, and became active in their parish, including serving as eucharistic ministers. Knowing that God desires not to lose a single soul, I felt there is no greater gift than knowing that my humble Web site has helped someone find his way back to God.

In addition to my Web site, I have been inspired to write a book about Medjugorje called *Medjugorje Investigated.* The idea germinated when I was watching a segment of "Inside Edition," a TV magazine program. In this particular segment, host Bill O'Reilly traveled to Medjugorje to investigate the claims of apparitions. During his report, O'Reilly did an interview with David Anderson, the ambassador to Yugoslavia when the apparitions first started in 1981. The ambassador (now deceased) told O'Reilly that the State Department requested that he send political officers to Medjugorje to see if there was any truth to what was being claimed there. Anderson sent two political officers to investigate, one of whom was a former priest. The officers' report was affirmative. This information sparked my interest because I couldn't imagine why the State Department would have an interest in religious happenings since our country's law mandates a separation of church and state. Thus began my quest to obtain State Department documents under the Freedom of Information Act. *Medjugorje Investigated* is a unique look at the apparitions through scientific studies and U.S. State Department documents that have been declassified for the book. It looks not only at the spiritual side of the apparitions, but also at the political upheaval surrounding these events by governments and Church officials.

Once again this is a blessing that I would never have dreamed possible. I've learned that God's gifts do not necessarily come in the form that we want them to, and we need to pray that we recognize them when they do come our way. I thank God for allowing me to play a small part in His great plan and I hope I will always remain a devoted and committed son to earn yet another coin for the Master.

Michael Kenneth Jones, Massachusetts

"Dear children! Today I invite you to give thanks to God for all the gifts you have discovered in the course of your life and even for the least gift that you have perceived. I give thanks with you and want all of you to experience the joy of these gifts. And I want God to be everything for each one of you. And then, little children, you can grow continuously on the way of holiness. Thank you for responding to my call."
Message of September 25, 1989

Peace

"Dear children! Today I invite
you to peace. I have come here as the
Queen of Peace and I desire to enrich you with
my motherly peace. Dear children, I love you and I
desire to bring all of you to the peace which only God
gives and which enriches every heart. I invite you to
become carriers and witnesses of my peace to this unpeace-
ful world. Let peace reign in the whole world, which is
without peace and longs for peace. I bless you with my
motherly blessing. Thank you for having responded to
my call."

Message of July 25, 1990

18
Make Me a Channel

I got to know Kathy when she agreed to chauffeur her mother-in-law and two elderly neighborhood ladies to a prayer group of which I was a member. The only thing I knew about her was that she was one of several corporate wives who had relocated to Plano, Texas, from New York. None of us noticed at the time that this attractive woman, awkwardly fumbling with the plastic rosary beads someone had handed her, was not a Catholic. Nor did we have any idea of the pain that she carried inside. Kathy would tell us later that the warmth and friendliness of our prayer group impressed her. She felt peaceful when she was with us, a much-needed peace, we discovered, when she eventually shared her story with us.

In 1987, while still living in New York, Kathy began to hemorrhage so severely that she took herself to the doctor, thinking perhaps that she was suffering from a miscarriage. After her examination and some tests the doctor called Kathy to her office. She appeared to be upset. "You will have to see a specialist," the doctor said softly. Kathy's mind began to wander and she was only half listening until she heard the word *cancer*. She straightened up in her chair unable to conceal her anxiety. "Mrs. Jones, did you hear what I said? You have cancer of the cervix." Like a mal-functioning computer, Kathy's mind was incapable of processing the data it had just been fed. "I am afraid Huntington Hospital is not equipped to handle your case."

Kathy couldn't remember the drive home. As she pulled up to the house, she slumped over the steering wheel and tried to piece together the events of the dreadful day. Finally, she raised her head and began to carefully examine the front of her house—her dream house—a dream that had been safely tucked away in her heart long before it became a reality. Was it only yesterday that she was trying (unsuccessfully) to adjust to the bitter disappointment of a corporate transfer, which meant leaving the Victorian house she and her husband had lovingly remodeled, to go to Texas? And, now, here she was, faced with the far more tragic news of having to fight for her very life. It was beyond her ability to endure.

As could be predicted, Kathy's husband Ed, a lawyer, approached their problem with the zeal of a crusader. He made it his mission to seek out the very best advice available. After carefully weighing all options, they chose Dr. Beckman, a surgeon who was affiliated with New York University Medical Center. The night before surgery was the most terrifying night of Kathy's life. She had to suffer all the pre-op indignities that left her feeling weak and nauseous. She finally fell asleep only to be awakened at 5:30 a.m. and told her surgery had been rescheduled: she was to go immediately. Kathy remembered calling out to God but it was more in desperation than actual prayer. As she lay on the gurney outside her room, nurses were busily walking up and down the corridor and occasionally one would stop and attempt to comfort her. It didn't help. While they were wheeling Kathy downstairs, she began to sob. It kept getting worse as she grappled with the possibility that she might not return. Kathy could not bear the thought of her husband being left alone to raise three daughters. From that moment until long after her treatment, the idea that God would help her simply did not exist.

Never having experienced surgery before, Kathy was shocked at how painful her recovery was. Dr. Beckman was optimistic about how the procedure had gone, but they had to wait for the pathology report to be absolutely certain. A few days passed when Dr. Beckman's assistant came into Kathy's room. Written all over his face was the same discomfort that she had observed in the doctor who first told her about the cancer. He said that two out of the thirteen lymph nodes that were removed during surgery proved to be cancerous. Kathy was totally unprepared for this news and immediately began to sink emotionally. Because she was young and strong, he recommended the highest level dosage of chemotherapy her body could tolerate.

The treatment was horrendous. They had to continually place ice packs around Kathy's body to control the fever that had spiked to 104 degrees. She concluded that death could not be worse than what she was going through. From the depths of her soul, Kathy pleaded with God to give her inner peace and the ability to accept her fate. She had never prayed more fervently. In fact, for the next few days she waited in anticipation for God's answer but there was no change. The anguish continued and, if anything, it increased. Kathy felt forgotten and completely abandoned. She could only conclude that prayer did not work; it was simply wishful thinking.

Although Kathy had given up on her own prayer, there was an enormous outpouring of prayer on her behalf, not only from loved ones, but from people she didn't even know.

Her aunt called her long distance every day to pray with her and tell her how much God loved her. Kathy had no more faith in her aunt's prayers than in her own, but this love and concern profoundly touched her. Kathy's brother-in-law, a Lutheran minister, had everyone in his church praying and he even prevailed upon the Catholic nuns across the street from his parish to pray for her as well. Her closest childhood friend, Linda, a talented artist who designed sets for theater, ballet, and movies, was busy working on a film for the Public Broadcasting Service (PBS) in New Jersey when she learned of Kathy's illness. Every day after shooting, she had her driver bring her to the hospital so she could visit her friend. On one such visit, Linda told Kathy that she began every day with prayer. In all the years they had been friends, Linda had never once talked about God. It was such a revelation to Kathy, especially coming at a time when she had dismissed prayer as an exercise in futility.

In December, Kathy was hospitalized for the second and final round of chemotherapy and even though it made her just as sick, her attitude had improved. She remembered watching the poison move through the tube into her veins and thinking how good it was that she had enough confidence to send Christmas cards. During this period, she also began radiation that drained her body of all its energy. These treatments were compounded by the fact that when they were over, Kathy and her husband had to prepare for their move to Texas. It was hard enough to give up the house she cherished, but to leave the support of family and dear friends...Kathy wondered how she would ever survive.

The Wednesday afternoon Rosary group Kathy had stumbled upon in Plano provided her with an unexpected sense of peace for a few precious hours each week and she looked forward to each gathering. One day Kathy overheard some of the women discussing a village in Yugoslavia where the Blessed Virgin Mary was reportedly appearing. It intrigued her that people were talking so matter-of-factly about the Mother of God appearing somewhere in the world in this day and age. The same day she learned that a man named Wayne Weible, a Lutheran like herself, had made several pilgrimages to this village named Medjugorje. A few weeks later, one of the women handed her Wayne's book, but she never seemed to find the time to read it.

Weeks passed and friends of Kathy and Ed came to visit. They had also undergone a personal crisis, as the wife had been diagnosed with Multiple Sclerosis. As they were talking, the woman noticed the book on the kitchen desk. "I know about that place," she said. "In fact, when you were in the hospital with cancer, a woman in my MS support group went to Medjugorje and I gave her a petition to pray for you." This news stunned Kathy because her friend wasn't even Catholic. It also made her wonder. Perhaps this chain of prayers, from friends and family in New York to strangers in a remote village in Yugoslavia, really had been heard. One thing became clear: she would read Wayne Weible's book as soon as possible.

Ironically, before Kathy began the book, she discovered that the author would be speaking in Dallas and she decided to attend. That night, she felt as if he were speaking directly to her heart. When the talk was over, she told Wayne briefly of her struggle with cancer and how she had recently learned that she had been prayed for in Medjugorje. Grasping her hand, he smiled, assuring her that she would be fine. He then reached into his pocket and placed a medal in her palm, saying it was blessed by Our Lady and she wanted him to give it to Kathy.

After finishing the book, Kathy was convinced that she had to go to Medjugorje. The ladies in the Rosary group advised her to pray about it and trust that God would get her there if it was meant to be. Kathy had not totally over-come her doubt about the efficacy of prayer, but she approached God as honestly as she could. "Lord, please give me a sign if I am supposed to go." Like an impatient child, she began looking for signs everywhere, but none appeared. Then, one Sunday after Mass, Ed pointed to a blurb in the church bulletin about a pilgrimage to Medjugorje. "I thought I might call and find out about this," he said. Kathy almost fell to the floor. This was her sign! Before she could catch her breath they were making arrangements to join a parish pilgrimage slated to leave Dallas on October 1. The pilgrimage would include a stop in Italy to visit the home-town of St. Francis of Assisi. Kathy borrowed a book on this popular saint so she could know as much about him as pos-sible. She couldn't remember the exact moment it happened, but the song of St. Francis, "Make Me a Channel of Your Peace," came into her head and would not leave.

On Saturday of the pilgrimage, Kathy's group boarded a bus for St. Elijah's Church where Fr. Jozo Zovko was pastor. The church was packed and Kathy positioned herself for a clear view for her video camera. When Father Jozo spoke, Kathy felt as if she were listening to God. The man exuded such holiness it was palpable. At the end of his talk, Father Jozo invited every priest present to go through the crowd and bless the people. The priests began milling through the crowd and Father Jozo left the altar and came down among the people to bless anyone who stood before him. To watch people who were standing perfectly normal one minute suddenly fall back on their heels the next struck Kathy as bizarre. She was convinced they were doing this to themselves in a burst of emotionalism. People were rushing to get near to Father Jozo and both Kathy and Ed found this distasteful; it reminded them of concert fans pushing just to get a glimpse of a rock star.

In spite of this, Ed urged Kathy to get Father Jozo's blessing, but she just couldn't force herself to join the throng. She had just finished folding up the tripod for the camera when a stranger walked up to her, put his hand on her elbow, and starting maneuvering her through the crowd. She tried to resist shouting, "You don't understand, I can't do this!" But the man wouldn't take no for an answer. Kathy turned around looking at Ed to rescue her but he motioned for her to go ahead. Then Kathy realized that the man who had created this situation had disappeared. Suddenly, Father Jozo was right in front of her. Kathy closed her eyes as he placed his hand over her head. She knew she was going to fall back but it was beyond her power to prevent it. Someone caught her and placed her gently on the floor. She began to experience a strange feeling in her hands and her head. Kathy tried to calm herself, but the feeling only intensified. It was like a pounding electrical current going through her in a circular motion. She had the impression that this power was shooting out of her and coming back into her body. There was no sense of time but Kathy found out later that she had been on the floor for about twenty-five minutes. At one point, thinking she might be ill, Ed placed his hand underneath the back of his wife's head and began to stroke the side of her face. The translator who assisted Father Jozo assured Ed that Kathy would be fine. Although she was completely aware of her surroundings, the only thing Kathy could do was concentrate on the unbelievable feeling in her body. She felt as if she were in a furnace in the midst of a roaring blaze, yet the fire did not hurt her. In fact, it felt wonderful.

When she opened her eyes for the third time, Kathy saw Ed standing up at the altar and Father Jozo was blessing him. He did not go down like his wife did, but his back and arms were shaking as if an electrical shock was going through him. Kathy closed her eyes once more. After a while, she became aware of people leaving the church. With the help of another person, Ed got her up and they went over and sat down in a pew. The feeling of heat had left, but Kathy still felt a pulsating sensation in her palms and fingers. Unlike the heat, this feeling was external and so real she had to open her eyes to see if someone was squeezing her hands. At that moment, the people in the church began to sing "Make Me a Channel of Your Peace," that beautiful melody that had haunted Kathy throughout the trip. She wanted to join in the singing, but she was so choked up that her voice cracked on every syllable.

As they made their way back to the bus, Kathy was greeted with smiles from the group. One of the women explained that her experience had been a "slaying in the Spirit." Kathy remembered thinking how odd it was that there were words to describe what had just happened. Others on the bus began to share their encounters, yet no one described anything as intense as Kathy had experienced. Kathy told the woman privately about the strange feeling she had in her hands and about the song of St. Francis. The woman smiled. "Perhaps, Kathy, it was St. Francis himself holding your hands."

Our prayer group back in Plano had been following Kathy's itinerary in Medjugorje closely and we offered prayers for her each day of the pilgrimage. The day after her return, Kathy came to my house to tell us about her trip. Although she was physically exhausted, there was a glow about her and talking about her experience seemed to energize her. Why God had singled Kathy out for such a magnificent display of the power of the Holy Spirit was something she did not pretend to understand. Her description of the feeling of heat and electricity sounded to us like a physical healing, but we kept our opinions to ourselves to let God reveal that to her in His own way.

As often happens with the passage of time, Kathy underwent a period of doubting what had actually happened in Medjugorje. Fortunately, God did not allow her to flounder for very long. In time He helped her to put the pieces together. She recalled being in the hospital back in New York and how her desperate search for peace of mind was almost as terrible as the cancer itself. She thought about her move to Plano and the unlikely situation of stumbling into a Catholic prayer group. She especially remembered how the peace that had eluded her in that hospital bed completely enveloped her the day she started to pray the Rosary. Kathy began to sense God's hand in her life. She had asked Him for peace and He gave it to her through the intercession of His mother.

Shortly after, Kathy felt God calling her to share in the full deposit of the faith by joining the Catholic Church. After enrolling in RCIA, her faith deepened with each passing day and she continued to grow in her affection for St. Francis, wondering if he hadn't taken her under his wing long before she was ever aware of his existence. In time Kathy realized that she had been healed physically in Medjugorje but, more importantly, she was healed spiritually.

On the Easter vigil in 1991, Kathy joined the Church, taking the name Francis of Assisi.

In time she was asked to consider becoming a eucharistic minister. The idea of holding the Body of Christ in her hands terrified her, but she knew she could not refuse. It wasn't long before God began placing Kathy in situations and circumstances where she could reach out and touch others with His love. Today He sends her to the bedside of others who, like herself, have been stricken with catastrophic illnesses. As they face eternal life, Kathy shares their moments of fear and doubt, to offer comfort and positive assurance that God loves them beyond all telling. Best of all, she is able to feed these dying souls with the Bread from heaven. Through His magnificent grace, Kathy has personally witnessed many brothers and sisters in the faith experience the same peace God gave to her: truly, the peace that surpasses all understanding.

Marion Lee, Maryland

"Dear children! I call you, little children, to pray without ceasing. If you pray, you are closer to God and He will lead you on the way of peace and salvation. That is why I call you today to give peace to others. Only in God is there true peace. Open your hearts and become those who give a gift of peace and others will discover peace in you and through you and in this way you will witness God's peace and love, which He gives you. Thank you for having responded to my call." Message of January 25, 2000

19

Instruments of Peace

I was born into a Catholic family in Lodz, Poland, a large industrial city with nearly one million inhabitants. My parents loved me very much and took me to church every Sunday. When I was about eighteen years old, however, I realized that my faith was that of a child and that it was no longer enough. I wanted love in my life, but I futilely sought it in the wrong places. For several months there was a fierce interior battle in my soul. I knew I could find my answers in God, yet I was afraid of Him. I feared He would want me to do something that was too hard, and I was not yet ready to completely change my life. During this time I tried to read Catholic books about love and faith. I spent some time trying to read the Bible, but the words did not penetrate my heart. Scripture became boring for me, as did the Eucharist, and I felt a deep void in my life.

Some of my closest classmates began to attend a charismatic renewal prayer group in the Jesuit church in my city, and I listened to their animated conversations about God and prayer. I saw how they believed that Jesus was close to them and I longed for the happiness they experienced. Finally, I decided to attend this prayer group with my friends and about forty other teenagers. The priest celebrated the Eucharist in such a special way that I understood for the first time each important word of the liturgy. It was on this day, after months of spiritual battle, that I decided for the first time in my life to say "yes!" to God. I offered Him my whole life and I immediately felt His love and peace in my heart. I was immeasurably happy and could not help falling in love. Remarkably, I began to understand the books I had been struggling with, especially the Bible, and I found myself with a strong desire to pray.

It wasn't long after I joined this prayer group that I learned of Medjugorje. I read many books about it and watched several videos. There was no other place in the world that I desired to go more, but there was a war going on at the time and my mother would not permit me. Some time later, during the winter, I attended a Taizé ecumenical youth meeting in Europe. As I prayed with about seventy thousand to eighty thousand other youths, I happened to run into a group of Croatians from the Medjugorje area. The leader of this group talked with such love about Our Lady and her messages. It turned out to be Mario Mijatovic, the man who would one day marry the visionary Vicka. Mario told me that if Gospa (as the locals lovingly refer to the Blessed Mother) invites me to Medjugorje, it is certain I will go. This fueled my desire even more. Finally, that spring, I convinced my mother to allow me to travel to Medjugorje if I took my father along with me.

My pilgrimage was filled with many blessings. I had already fallen in love with the Lord and now Medjugorje helped me to love Our Lady. It instilled a deep sense of peace and joy in my heart, and an even stronger desire for prayer, especially the Rosary. Like many others, I returned home a changed person. I was determined to maintain my conversion, but as the years passed I permitted the effects of Medjugorje to lessen. Then, my mother died of cancer. This loss and other sudden changes left me once again in a spiritual desert. My desire to pray and receive the Eucharist greatly diminished, but I forced myself anyway. During this crisis of faith, I felt so far away from God. Looking back, I think perhaps He wanted to show me how weak I was without Him.

The Blessed Mother, meanwhile, did not forget her daughter. One day, I was searching the Internet and decided to return to a Web site about Medjugorje that I had often visited in the past. This time I felt compelled to sign up to join the Queen of Peace Prayer Group. Here I discovered more than two thousand people from around the world trying to live Our Lady's messages. It is a group that prays for each other and cares for one another, bonded by a common goal and the grace of the Holy Spirit. Through the example of these people, I have learned to love God and Our Lady once more and the messages have become alive for me. The prayer group also brought me together with a very special friend, Carolanne Kilichowski from America, whom I believe God has placed in my life for very special reasons.

Carolanne is of Polish descent, and she had responded to an invitation to sponsor someone in another country to receive a newsletter about Medjugorje. She was given my name. Beginning with my first e-mail to thank her, we have communicated constantly and have become fast friends. Our common heritage, our love for Our Lady, and our oneness in spiritual matters bonded us immediately. One day I told Carolanne that my mother had died of cancer on July 29, 2002. Carolanne told me that July 29 was her birthday and while she realized that she could never replace my own mother, she offered to love me as her own daughter and promised to always be there for me. My heart melted.

I had the wonderful experience of meeting Carolanne and her husband when they attended a pilgrimage in Poland. We both know that God has put this relationship together for His purpose and we are truly enjoying each other in prayer and friendship.

Carolanne and I both feel called to do God's work together and our current project is raising awareness and support for a special school system in Poland called "Queen of Peace School." It was the desire awakened in Medjugorje of Father Eugeniusz Spiolek, a Pijarist monk who is very devoted to Our Lady. He created the first school in Lowicz, Poland, after much prayer and discernment, and plans to create more schools like these in other places. There are state schools, of course, but Father feels called to create environments that will teach children how to pray with the heart and live Our Lady's messages. He sees how strongly evil attacks children in our world and believes that these schools devoted to Our Lady Queen of Peace can counteract that. Father recognizes that the future depends on our youth and if we can instill belief and desire in our children, the mission of Our Lady will continue.

Jesus Christ is the central figure at the Queen of Peace school, where everything is focused on God's providence. The chapel is at the heart of the school and the classes are constructed around it. The teachers have created a beautiful spirit of community by developing wonderful relationships with their pupils, and they pray together every day, including a morning Rosary. When I visited the school for the first time, I could sense the peace and happiness that existed there, and I hope that one day my own children will be able to attend such a beautiful school.

When Father Eugeniusz started the school, he had no money. He entrusted his needs to Our Lady and she did not disappoint: people came forth with what he needed at the proper time. Not long ago, Father received the gift of a

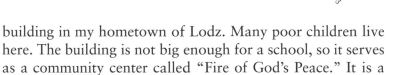

building in my hometown of Lodz. Many poor children live here. The building is not big enough for a school, so it serves as a community center called "Fire of God's Peace." It is a place where children can come after school, a "second home" where they and their families can find peace of heart, especially the poorest families afflicted by addiction, unemployment, poverty, and other difficulties.

With an ocean between us, Carolanne in America and I in Poland are uniting efforts to solicit help in creating more "Queen of Peace" schools and "Fire of God's Peace" communities in the places where God wills them to be—eventually, we hope, around the world. Our dream is that these places will help children, especially those without hope, to open their hearts to the call of Our Lady in Medjugorje in order to live her messages. Prayer is needed foremost for this endeavor, as well as material help in order for this dream to be a reality, because times are hard in Poland and many people are out of work. My American friend and I feel blessed to do what we can to support this effort to help spread the messages that our heavenly Mother teaches in Medjugorje, the ultimate school of love and peace.

Anna Karczemska, Poland

"Dear children! Also today, joy is in my heart. I desire to thank you for making my plan realizable. Each of you is important, therefore, little children, pray and rejoice with me for every heart that has converted and become an instrument of peace in the world. Prayer groups are powerful and through them I can see, little children, that the Holy Spirit is at work in the world. Thank you for having responded to my call." Message of June 25, 2004

20
People of Peace and Love

Although I was brought up Catholic and attended Catholic schools, I was never grounded in my faith. I had a hard time with the religious sisters at my school, who taught us that Catholics were the only ones going to heaven. This attitude hurt me, because most of the friends I had growing up were not Catholic. I thought to myself, "What kind of God is this that won't allow my friends to get to heaven?" I did not experience God's love in church; instead, what left its impression on me were rules and discipline. The Latin language of the liturgy also made it difficult for me to understand the real meaning of the Mass and the Eucharist.

The influence of the 1960s and the changes brought about by Vatican II did not help my faith much and, in a foolish move, I eloped at the age of twenty and got married in a little chapel called "Doves of Happiness." Unfortunately, my marriage was anything but happy. It didn't take me long to realize that I had made a big mistake and that my marriage was falling apart. Desperate, I sought the help of the pastor of a local church. When he discovered where I had been married, he told me I was a sinner and turned me away. After that, I wanted nothing more to do with the Catholic Church. I would seek meaning to my life through other faith expressions such as Islam, Buddhism, Jehovah's Witnesses, Latter Day Saints, and Pentecostals. All of them had some good qualities and all claimed to love Jesus, but none of them gave me the fulfillment I was seeking.

My marriage ended after seven years, but not before blessing me with a son, Cully, and a daughter, Nikki. I had them both baptized in the Catholic Church, although I did not raise them in the faith. Perhaps it was the prompting of the Holy Spirit from my own infant baptism that led me to have my children receive this sacrament. In any event, it ended up being providential. When Cully was in sixth grade at the public school, his grades were rather poor and he was getting into trouble. There was a Catholic school around the corner from where we were living and I thought he might get a better education and more discipline there. Since my children were baptized Catholics, I transferred both of them. My daughter, who was preparing for First Holy Communion and First Reconciliation, began asking me to come to Mass with her. I had no interest whatsoever. She persisted until I finally agreed. To my surprise, church was completely different from what I had remembered. There was love in this liturgical celebration, a love that I could feel. I decided to read more about the sacraments that my children were receiving and I became more involved with the parish, even teaching Confirmation so I could continue to learn more about my rediscovered faith.

After my children left home for college, my motivation to go to Mass began to wane. Church started to lose its appeal for me and other things began to take priority in my life. At first I would skip an occasional Sunday Mass and then it would be a more frequent occurrence. Eventually I found myself a holidays-only Catholic. It seemed I didn't really need the Mass or the sacraments. I had always believed in Jesus Christ since I was a small child and I taught my children to know and love Jesus as well. Surely I would go to heaven for that.

In March of 2000, my son and I had a falling out. He had met a girl in college who I felt was not a good influence. In particular, I was unhappy about them smoking marijuana. The argument came to a head one day, and Cully cursed at me and ran out of the house. We didn't speak for months. I decided to let him go, convincing myself that he would come back when he was ready. In the back of my mind, however, I had an uneasy feeling that something bad was going to happen. Therefore, I was relieved when our communication began to open again through an occasional letter.

One spring morning I was sitting in my backyard in California, gazing at the snow-capped mountains in the distance. It was a favorite spot of mine to meditate and put my mind in a quiet place. I dozed off for a few moments and during that brief slumber I saw a white church with a steeple and a cross on top and green grass all around. I wasn't quite sure what to make of this dream. Two days later I received a religious Mother's Day card from my son. On the cover was a church similar to the one I had dreamt about two days earlier. It was unusual for Cully to send me a serious card, especially a religious one.

The following month, in June, I went out to my backyard on a beautiful night after saying some prayers and set up my telescope as I often liked to do. While adjusting the focus, I spotted a shining white cross way up on one of the mountains. It struck me as odd that I had never noticed it before, and that I seemed to be the only person able to see it, with or without the telescope.

By September, a package arrived in the mail for me. I had placed a blind bid on the Internet for a certified painting by artist Thomas Kinkade, although I did not know which painting it was. When I opened the package I was amazed to discover a picture of a church with a steeple and a white cross on top and lots of green grass. I decided this must have been the reason for the church-related dream and Mother's Day card.

On October 10, 2000, I woke up at six o'clock in the morning and then fell right back to sleep. I drifted off and found myself talking to someone, although I didn't know who. The person said to me, "I have someone here who wants to see you." I thought perhaps it was my father or grandfather, who had passed away. When I turned around, however, I was surprised to see my son, Cully. We hadn't spoken in months and I demanded to know what he was doing here. I even started to tell the person accompanying us what my son had done to me. My son interrupted by grabbing my hand and saying. "Mom, I died." I couldn't believe what he was saying to me. "I died, Mom," he continued. "I was in a car accident. I only came back because I had to tell you that I'm sorry and I love you." My body seemed to go into convulsions and I began to scream, but I couldn't wake myself no matter how hard I tried. I'm not sure what happened next or how much time transpired, but the next thing I know I was holding hands with my son and I was at peace. He was asking me if I was going to be okay. I felt so incredibly happy. Cully told me he had to go back. We embraced and kissed goodbye. I woke up with a great big smile on my face because I was sure that this dream meant that my son and I were going to get back together again. My prodigal son was coming home.

I was on cloud nine when the telephone rang and a voice on the other end told me I had better sit down; there was bad news. I responded, "You are *not* calling to tell me that my son is dead!" But it was true—he had been killed in a car accident during the night. I begged the caller to tell me that it wasn't true, but I knew in my heart that it was. Cully had come to tell me first. I was in shock, and like a zombie I began calling family and friends. On October 17, the day of my son's funeral, my eyes saw for the first time the church in which we were going to have my son's service. It was located at the cemetery and was surrounded by green grass. There was a cross and a steeple on top.

After my son's death, my whole life seemed to be a living hell. Nothing could be worse than the loss of a child, not even hell itself. I couldn't believe that God had done this to me. I had tried to be a good Catholic and a good parent, and this was my reward? My friends told me to talk to God about it, but He was the last one I wanted to talk to. I closed the door on everything and everyone and didn't go anywhere. I stopped working and did nothing but cry and visit the cemetery. In my bitterness, I refused to talk to anyone, even my daughter, who was away at college. I felt completely alone, and that's what I wanted.

My daughter Nikki, feeling abandoned, felt that she needed something to fill the void in her life. Six months after my son's death, she became pregnant. On December 3, 2001, she gave birth to my beautiful grandson Caleb, who was born with serious medical problems. It was unknown if he would even survive. The tiny child stayed in the hospital until he was four months old, fighting for his life. I feared the thought of him dying and the suffering that it would put Nikki through. No one should ever have to live with the constant pain I was suffering. I would visit my grandson daily and just stare at him, feeling completely helpless. Finally, I decided that I had to do something, so I bought a rosary at the gift shop and began reciting this prayer to him daily. I didn't even know how to say the Rosary; I just read the prayer from a little booklet that came with it.

In May 2002, my grandson was released from the hospital. Although this was joyful news, it did not alleviate the slow death process I still seemed to be going through. I had no one to talk to that could possibly understand my pain. I was an alien to the world and upset with God for taking my son. When June rolled around again I was sitting out in my yard. I was not praying; I was just thinking about dying. Suddenly, it got very still outside and I heard a voice that is impossible for me to describe. At that moment, I felt the presence of the Blessed Mother. She spoke to me and said, "*I understand what you are feeling. I, too, have felt the pain of losing a child. I lost my child Jesus. I saw my Son carry a cross while people laughed and spit on Him. I saw men put nails in His hands and head and saw the blood and sweat run down from His face. I saw my Son suffer and die on the same cross He carried for the life of the world. And while He was suffering, I was suffering. I begged my Father to allow me to trade places. I was in pain and agony and with every passing day I grieved as I thought about the memories of His death and how I missed Him. There wasn't anything I could do—it was my Father's will. So my child, I do feel and understand your pain. And yes, your son has died and you will miss him, but remember, because of my Son's death, my Son, Jesus, made it possible for your son to live again. So don't be angry with Our Lord. Love my Son as He loves Cully and you. Praise Him for the gift He gave the world.*"

I dropped to my knees in a torrent of emotion, realizing suddenly that I *did* have someone who understood my pain and suffering and that I had been selfish in turning away from God and blaming Him. I couldn't stop crying and I begged Blessed Mary and her Son for their forgiveness for my lack of trust.

As healing and understanding began to enter my life, I knew that I needed some time away from home. I had always loved the movie *Song of Bernadette* about the visionary of Lourdes, so I started looking on the Internet for pilgrimages to that shrine. Instead, I discovered information about Medjugorje. I had heard of Medjugorje about ten years earlier, but I had no interest back then. That evening, I stayed up all night reading about the apparitions and Our Lady's messages and the next day I called to make travel plans. There was a cancellation on the June pilgrimage, and somehow I was able to get my passport in just a few short weeks. Everything seemed to fall into place perfectly for me. I was still on an emotional high from the fact that the Blessed Mother herself had come to comfort me and that I wasn't alone anymore. Finally, I had a friend who understood a mother's loss of a son.

Our bus entered Medjugorje on June 20 and tears came to my eyes when I saw atop one of the mountains a shining white cross. It was exactly two years from the time I first saw the cross from my backyard in California. From the moment I saw the cross and arrived at the house where I would be staying in Medjugorje, I had already made an incredible conversion of heart. That week there were many tears, but there was also unbelievable joy. I didn't tell anyone in the group what I had suffered and they would never have guessed because I was always happy and full of energy. My fellow travelers were completely unaware that I had lost my son eighteen months before, that I had become antisocial and a prisoner to my home, and that I had a serious grieving condition that was slowly debilitating me. At the same time, no one knew about my conversion because it happened so fast. I didn't realize it myself, because I was so in tune with each moment of the pilgrimage and enjoying the closeness of God. I had never felt this kind of peace or love in my entire life; this was the peace I had been searching for even before my son's death. In Medjugorje, I became alive again.

When I returned home from my pilgrimage, I again felt like a fish out of water. I found I could no longer return to the life I once had. I said to God, "I promise, I am giving You my life from this day forward. I am going to be a worker for You. I'm turning everything over to You and entrusting You to guide me. My life is Yours." I wasn't exactly sure how to go about carrying out this promise, so I started by going to Mass every morning as I had done in Medjugorje. I even started talking to priests and sisters about my conversion, but they didn't really understand my zealous love for Jesus and the Blessed Mother. I couldn't find one person that had the kind of fire that was burning inside of me.

Although I felt a renewed desire to return to work, I knew that I could no longer perform my job as a paralegal working primarily on divorce cases. I could no longer in good conscience help men and women dissolve their marriages. Somehow, I knew that God would provide. It was then that I decided to get involved in hospice to work with people who were about to face death. I also signed up for religious classes to nurture my spiritual growth. About eighteen months later, I was on a retreat with the Carmelite sisters when I recognized a call to the religious life. I had never considered this before. I just assumed that I had chosen my vocation as wife and mother and there was no "second" life.

I began to research different orders, visiting convents and staying overnight. But I was often turned away from religious orders because I was in my forties, I had been married, and I was a mother. This surprised me. If God had put a desire in my heart to serve Him as a sister, who were these people to say no? Even if I wasn't right for their particular order, they should have supported me on my journey. In time I began to wonder if I had made a mistake about having a calling.

It was then I discovered through an Internet search a religious order called the Sisters of the Sick Poor of Los Angeles. Established in 2003, it is a contemporary community of Catholic women drawn together out of compassion and love to serve the sick, poor, and marginalized, as an off-shoot of the Friars of the Sick Poor of Los Angeles. The more I read about this order, the more it intrigued me. I liked the work they did and the fact that women could be older or even disabled and be welcomed by this community. I also liked that the sisters wore habits. This was important to me, as I wanted a uniform that would tell people proudly that I belonged to Jesus.

After my trip to Medjugorje, material things no longer meant anything to me. Therefore, when I began searching for religious orders, I was willing to give up my possessions. If an order required me to be cloistered, I would do that happily. The Sisters of the Sick Poor, however, are a self-supporting order. The sisters have the freedom to live individually and have their own jobs. That meant I could keep my home and continue my work for Hospice. Everything seemed to feel right to me about this order and it took only one visit to realize that I had found the right one—this is where Jesus wanted me to be. I applied and was accepted.

The Sisters of the Sick Poor of Los Angeles profess four vows: poverty, chastity, obedience, and self-sustenance, which calls us to be responsible and good stewards of our own finances. We feed the poor and the homeless in downtown Los Angeles, providing them with food and clothing. We also minister to the sick in hospitals. Because the order allows a sister to apply her skills in work areas in which she feels comfortable, I am encouraged to continue my work with Hospice. I take religious education classes at the archdiocese and eventually I will be taking Clinical Pastor Education classes to get my license to work as a minister in counseling. I think I would like to get involved in grief counseling to help bring God's healing grace to those who suffer the loss of a loved one. On February 11, the feast of the apparitions at Lourdes, I made my temporary vows and received my habit as a bride of Christ. I did not choose this date; it was assigned to me. I take it as confirmation from my favorite saint, Bernadette, that I am on the right path.

I still have, as a souvenir from my pilgrimage to Medjugorje, five stones with the main messages of the apparitions—Prayer, Fasting, Eucharist, Confession, and Holy Scripture—printed on them. It amazes me how all of these aspects to my spirituality have deepened since they were planted in my soul a few years ago. My prayer life, for example, has really blossomed. In addition to praying the Hours as a religious, my communication with Christ and His Mother is wonderful. Also part of my spiritual expression is daily Mass, monthly Confession, and routine fasting. Holy scripture especially has come alive for me in a new, more meaningful way and I find the Bible a pleasure to read now.

I particularly love the scripture verse from Isaiah (43:1) "Thus says the Lord who created you and formed you, fear not for I have called you by name. You are mine." This was a verse that my spiritual director gave me when I was discerning my vocation.

At my ceremony on February 11, I used this scripture verse on my invitation. Since the Blessed Mother's words and teachings from Medjugorje have become a definitive part of my life, I incorporated her words in my ceremony as well. One of her messages that has always touched me in a special way is the one in which she asks us to pray for those who do not yet know God's love, that their hearts may open and draw closer to her heart and the heart of her Son.

I'm not sure exactly where my spiritual journey will take me, particularly with the flexibility of my new order, but I will just take one step at a time and do my best. I know that God is not asking me to single-handedly save the world; He just wants me to do my part and show His love to others. Looking back, I see how Medjugorje has helped me with my healing and with the transformation my life continues to go through. I will always be grateful for the Sorrowful Mother who helped me turn my pain and suffering into peace and love for others.

Sister Anne Mitchell, California

"Dear children! Also today I call you to pray. Pray, little children, in a special way for all those who have not come to know God's love. Pray that their hearts may open and draw closer to my heart and the heart of my Son Jesus, so that we can transform them into people of peace and love. Thank you for having responded to my call."
Message of January 25, 2004

21
Food Where There Is Hunger

In 1993, I was watching television from my home in Manchester, UK, with my girlfriend at the time seated next to me. A news story came on about refugees fleeing the terrible fighting in a faraway place called Bosnia-Herzegovina. The two of us, in an instant, felt moved to do something immediately; these people needed our help now. Our first impulse was to get a van, fill it with food, and take it to Bosnia. In hindsight, I believe this unusual burst of humanitarianism was a moment of grace, a turning point after which my life would never be the same again.

Anxious not to let our conviction cool, we researched ways to carry out our rather naive mission. We read about other groups from various parts of the country that had the same idea of bringing supplies and assistance to this war-torn region, specifically to a place called Medjugorje, so we decided to join efforts with them. At the time, I was certainly not doing this for religious reasons. I would probably classify myself back then as a "baptized pagan," a person who showed up at church on Sunday, but whose lifestyle was far from being Christian. I was in this simply to help others.

We named our initiative "Manchester Medjugorje Appeal." The people who came together for this appeal did so for many reasons. Some had been to Medjugorje before and were profoundly affected, some were traditional Catholics, some were from other Christian churches, and still others were atheists acting solely on a humanitarian impulse. No one on the team had any experience of aid work, fundraising, or handling the myriad of difficulties we would face. We just took the first step and God took it from there.

Our first challenge was to find a place to store the food-stuffs that were collected from donors and churches in the area. We gained permission to use an old school building on the grounds of St. Alphonsus Roman Catholic Church in Old Trafford, Manchester. Next, we needed to start collecting food. We created a simple, handwritten poster and made pho-tocopies that were distributed to churches in the area along with large cardboard boxes. This publicity drew more volun-teers, and word began to spread about our organization.

Food began to flood in so fast that we couldn't pack it quickly enough. Deliveries arrived by the vanload from churches of all denominations and from all over the city— even as far as Cheshire and Derbyshire. Funds started to come in, too. In a surprising move, the local council gave us permission to conduct street collections citywide for three weekends in a row. With success, however, came new prob-lems. How could we get all of this food over to Bosnia? We wouldn't need a van; we would need a *fleet* of vans! As we pondered this dilemma, a new volunteer arrived with the answer. He was a landscape gardener at Manchester Airport where he had spotted a number of unused but operational vehicles rusting on the apron. He went to see the managing director of the airport and asked if we could use the vehicles to take our supplies to Bosnia. To our amazement, the man agreed, and after a few phone calls they were signed over to us, even filled with petrol. Since there wasn't a mechanic among us, we had to beg for help once again, and help was provided. A local garage carried out urgent repairs to one

van and the rest were given a thorough inspection and serv-
icing by the Territorial Army Transport Corps, whose base
was around the corner from our warehouse.

Despite all of these miracles, I was still oblivious to the
workings of God in our operations. I saw this simply as
people helping other people. We were going to deliver the
food and supplies and then I would move on with my life.
God, however, had other plans. And so, in that summer of
1993, we embarked on our sojourn to Medjugorje, loaded
down with food, toiletries, blankets, medical supplies, and
equipment. Once we arrived in Bosnia, we visited a refugee
camp the day after the refugees arrived. They had very little,
if anything, with them, and they were in poor health and
spirits. An old man approached us as we were unloading the
boxes of food. He had been forced to leave his home by sol-
diers and had been given only a few minutes to gather his
possessions. In the process he had lost his spectacles and
wondered if we happened to have any. As an after-thought,
just before we left England, we had packed a small box of
eyeglasses to fill an empty space. The man patiently rooted
through the box, trying on different pairs of spectacles until
he found a pair that was just right. He was filled with joy at
the gift of sight made possible by the simple donation of a
pair of discarded eyeglasses.

The trip was most rewarding and when we returned
home we were amazed to be greeted with more donations.
We began to realize that this trip would be the first of many,
and that there was something larger at work here. I believe
that we were led to Medjugorje for a special purpose beyond
bringing relief to the suffering refugees. We were called not
just to deliver, but to receive: to receive the grace to open our
hearts to God and find a profound sense of peace amidst the

chaos of the ensuing war. I say this because there was a real and profound change taking place among some of the volunteers. All around me I witnessed a change of heart, a newfound faith, or the renewal of a lukewarm faith. For some, it happened on their first trip to Medjugorje. For others, it was later. It would take me three trips to Medjugorje before the Lord could penetrate my stubborn heart. Fortunately, He and His mother are patient.

I credit Medjugorje as the catalyst in my conversion, turning me back to God and back to the sacramental life of the Church. It was Medjugorje that readied and inspired me to return to Confession after having spent all of my adult life away from it, which was a significant first step in my desire to be reconciled with the Lord. Through the sacraments, I discovered a peace I had not known before. My faith life was strengthened through prayer, fasting, and the Mass. It would be further fortified through baptism of the Holy Spirit, charismatic renewal, and reading the spiritual writings of God's chosen ones, particularly the inspirations of Matthew Kelly, a Catholic motivational speaker and author from Australia.

As our faith grew, so did our desire to continue helping God's people in need. By this point we had changed our name to "Medjugorje International Relief" to reflect a wider sphere of work, and our day and all its efforts were centered on prayer. Over the years we have been blessed to be able to work with other Medjugorje prayer groups around the country, uniting our efforts in work and prayer for an even greater good. We were still a bunch of amateurs, still in a shed in Old Trafford, and still relying on Divine Providence for all that we needed. As it is demonstrated in holy scripture, God chooses the weak, the least qualified, the inexperienced, and the barmy (crazy) to show His power and glory, and that is precisely what He did with us. Our philosophy was that "God softens the hearts and we simply pack the boxes, sign the checks, and direct traffic." Every six months we have an empty warehouse and an empty bank account to match, and then God fills them both up.

With each endeavor, God provides the extended hands we need. He gifts us with mechanics to service and repair convoy vehicles, journalists to publicize our work, typists to prepare literature, hospital workers to secure second-hand equipment, and people to pack supplies and blankets and obtain the necessary aid and financial support. Most of the aid we receive does not come from large corporate donations, but from individuals at churches, schools, synagogues, and mosques. The people who work at Medjugorje International Relief are simply volunteers and servants, working around regular jobs and family commitments. There are no salaries or expenses paid. We absorb the cost of stamps, envelopes, and phone calls so that every possible pound and donated item can go to those in need.

In the early 1990s, we were able to drive to Medjugorje in convoys (usually in donated vehicles) and deliver the aid into the hands of the refugees personally. As our activities continued over the years and opportunities came up to provide help in other countries, we began to work in partnership with other groups, particularly missionaries, and ship out supplies by lorry or container. The work has crossed all boundaries in that people of various Christian denominations, Muslim and Jewish communities, and those with no faith whatsoever, show solidarity with our brothers and sisters in need. Aid is distributed without regard to race or religion.

To date, Medjugorje International Relief has been able to send millions of pounds in aid to twenty-five countries throughout the world. Often it is in a small way, with one-time projects or donations, and sometimes it is more sustained work achieved over a number of years. To Bosnia and Croatia we have sent approximately sixty tons of food and toiletries, thirty-three tons of blankets and clothes, five ambulances, eight vans/minibuses for refugee camps, medical supplies for hospitals, and financing for rebuilding after the war. In Liberia, we were able to work with the Salesians and send two minibuses; twenty-nine tons of clothing and blankets; four thousand shoeboxes filled with gifts for children; and large quantities of new and used tools, typewriters, stationary, and sewing machines for training schools. We have sent money to modify the water system in the city jail at Manila in the Philippines. We funded part of the cost of a power station for a leper colony in China. We provided a month's worth of running costs for a women's support center (pro-life counseling) in Vladivostok in Eastern Russia. We have sponsored young people in India in their fees for further education. And we have supplied medical equipment to a hospital in Cuba and another in the Gambia, salvaged from a hospital in Manchester. For the past two years, much of our fundraising has been directed to the slave redemption program in the Sudan with our partner, Christian Solidarity International. On one recent mission, a boy and his grandmother were set free from slavery and the child declared that he wanted to become a Christian. We have witnessed many examples of such evangelization, including numerous requests to know more about Medjugorje, another indication that God is working actively through us.

Medjugorje International Relief, now in its twelfth year of operation, has not been the brainchild or credit of one person, but literally a cast of thousands. The significant driving force is not the volunteers but the One who inspires and leads us. It is His action that opens doors, paves the way, and softens hearts. It is He who dots the i's and crosses the t's in every aspect; we simply carry out the plan.

I believe that a big part of the essence of Medjugorje is a call to love our neighbor in a real and tangible way. As Our Lady says, we are called to bring love where there is hatred and food where there is hunger. God has shown us through this appeal that He can use anyone, anywhere, and do something splendid. Therefore, we must not be timid in being led by the Spirit to take new steps and begin new efforts, especially if we allow God to do the rest. Medjugorje International Relief is just one example of a practical walk with God that has yielded blessings beyond our wildest dreams because His vision is always greater than ours. With Him, all things are possible, if only we say "yes." In the end, what God has given us far outweighs what we have been able to give to His children: peace, joy, and yes, relief.

Steve Clark, England

"Dear children! Also, today, I call you to be love where there is hatred and food where there is hunger. Open your hearts, little children, and let your hands be extended and generous so that, through you, every creature may thank God the creator. Pray, little children, and open your heart to God's love, but you cannot if you do not pray. Therefore, pray, pray, pray. Thank you for having responded to my call."
Message of September 25, 2004

22
Community of Love

I grew up in the South with two values impressed upon my heart: a deep Catholic faith and a strong sense of family. Visiting my relatives in Italy as a teenager and witnessing their commitment as family and community made a great impression on me, and I came back committed to the idea that one day I would establish that kind of heritage in my home state of Alabama. I married my wife Annette, a convert to Catholicism, in 1975 and settled initially outside of Birmingham. A few years later, we found some wooded property in the remote hills of Sterrett on which to build a home. I was drawn to this land as soon as I laid eyes on it, and once we purchased it I offered it to God for His desires.

In 1981, the same year that the Blessed Mother began appearing in Medjugorje, Annette and I began construction on our house. I owned a landscaping/excavating company with about twenty-five employees, a business I had started myself, and it was against my nature to put myself in debt by taking out loans. Therefore, we worked on the house as money became available, even though it would take eight or nine years to reach completion.

My Catholic faith was ingrained in me from childhood, but it was a book I read about the apparitions of Fatima that ignited my love for the Blessed Mother. It affected me so deeply that I promised Our Lady if she ever appeared on the face of the earth again, I would be there to witness it.

Understandably then, when a close friend told me in 1984 that the Blessed Mother was appearing in Yugoslavia, my interest was piqued. A week later, a reporter covering the Winter Olympics in Sarajevo announced that a teenager had been arrested an hour away for claiming to see visions of the Virgin Mary, and it was causing an uprising among the population of that Communist nation. I was moved in my soul at this and I felt a need to investigate these apparitions for myself.

About two years later, Annette and I had started our family and our home was progressing nicely. I had an inner yearning at this time to give myself entirely to the Blessed Mother through a yearlong formal consecration. Among other prayers, I prayed the fifteen prayers of St. Bridget of Sweden every day with my two young sons. Although I worked long, hard hours, I managed to make this prayer commitment every day. During that year, my business was spread thin from financing several jobs, but at the completion of them the business turned around and our home was in its final stages of construction. I decided to take my family on a pilgrimage to Rome and Fatima with a two-day trip to Medjugorje in gratitude for our blessings. The year of prayers I had started was coming to an end while we were in Rome, so my sons and I entered the Church of St. Paul on the last day to complete them. We were astounded to discover that we were kneeling before the same crucifix at which St. Bridget received these prayers from the Lord over six hundred years ago. We could never have imagined such a grace to end the year of prayer, but I still prayed to be consecrated in a special way to Our Lady.

We had only planned two days in Medjugorje because we weren't completely sure if the apparitions were still occurring. In 1986, the apparitions were taking place in

Father Slavko Barberic's office/bedroom in the rectory. No one but priests and sisters and others with extraordinary circumstances were permitted in this room with the visionaries during the apparitions. Pilgrims would crowd outside, peering in the windows and pressing against the walls to hear what was going on. I found myself in the front of this throng of onlookers, not realizing how crowded it would be. When the door opened to allow the priests in, the crowd began pushing to get closer, and I was stunned when I was singled out of the crowd to come inside. I couldn't think of a better place in the world than to be consecrated to Our Lady just prior to her apparition. I turned to a priest and asked him privately if he would consecrate me to the Blessed Mother before the apparition started. He happened to be on our pilgrimage and knew that I was completing a year of prayer, so he invoked all fifteen priests in the room to circle around me and join him. It was a profound grace to be prayed over by these holy men of the Church. I was even more overwhelmed when the Blessed Mother appeared to the children, and I left the room afterward overcome with emotion.

I signed up to return to Medjugorje three months later because I still wasn't sure what was going on there, but I felt compelled to take another look. I witnessed powerful conversions and physical healings on this trip and I again ended up in the apparition room. There was a small part of me that had some doubts that these events might not be from God. Therefore, before I embarked on a third trip, I visited the Blessed Sacrament in my home parish to prepare for my pilgrimage. During prayer, a petition came to my heart and I wrote it down. "If it is God's will, we humbly ask that the conversion taking place in Medjugorje be allowed to take place here and that it divinely spread throughout the whole region."

On the way to Medjugorje, I prayed about the petition in my hand. I implored God that if this petition was not from Him, that He not allow it to be read in Medjugorje. But if it *was* from Him, I prayed that He would open the doors and let it be read directly to Our Lady. With this prayer, I felt at peace. During my time in Medjugorje, I looked for opportunities to present this petition. I spoke to several people who were close to the visionaries, including their friends and family, but no opportunity availed itself for a visionary to present my petition. On the last day of my pilgrimage, I was walking to St. James and concluded that God had answered my prayer about the petition: it was simply not His will. I released the matter into His hands and promised I would not lift a finger anymore to have it read. Just as I reached the church, an interpreter for Marija, one of the visionaries, ran up to me and said Marija had agreed to read the petition to Our Lady and that I was invited to come to the apparition room.

Once inside, the interpreter advised me that Marija had said not to be disappointed if Our Lady did not give me an answer. In the early years, the Blessed Mother patiently answered every question posed to her. But gradually she made it clear that it was time for people to stop asking questions and simply listen instead. To my delight, I was able to kneel right next to Marija as she went into ecstasy, but I was still determined to know for certain that this was not a deception from the devil. I prayed with all my might, saying to God, "If this is not from You, show that to me. I don't want to believe in something that is not from You—I need a sign. I need to understand that this is Our Lady appearing right here in front of me." As I was praying, I leaned over into the apparition and looked Marija in the eye. Suddenly, I felt something like an electric current run from my toes to my head, and a grace entered my heart in a powerful way that told me this was truly Our Lady appearing here. I was so firmly convicted that I knew at that moment I would die rather than deny the truth of Medjugorje.

After the vision, Marija got up and wrote something out on paper, which she handed to me. I couldn't believe I was getting an answer. The Croatian handwriting was translated for me. Our Lady said, *"Pray, and by your life witness. Not with words but rather through prayer will you attain what your desire is. Therefore, pray more and live in humility."*

I took this message home with me, marveling over every word, but I did not really understand what it meant. And so I began a period of real prayer and penance to unlock the mystery, during which I was inspired to start writing about Medjugorje, although I had never written before. At this point in my life I was thirty-three years old, with a wife and three children and a productive landscape and design business that I was planning to pass on to my sons one day. I loved my work and being outdoors, but I had the strong sense that God was calling me to follow Him in a different direction. I never had an ambition for ministry or for being locked up in an office writing, but at the same time I was growing willing and ready to turn my life over to God and work for Our Lady. The fact that I had no debt with my business enabled me to be able to walk away from it when God revealed the time.

There was a man who lived on the hill across the road from us and we both shared a love for the land and its history. When the man grew ill, I helped care for a large field of land that was adjacent to our house. The field was so beautiful that Annette and I had built our home to face it, and there was a peacefulness about the land that enabled me to go into deep prayer while riding my tractor on it. In the center of the field was a large lone evergreen tree. It obviously had survived all kinds of adverse weather conditions to be standing all by itself in such a large open area, so I figured there must be something special about it. My family loved to sit under this tree and picnic there. One afternoon I was inspired to ask for God's blessing on the tree to continue to protect it. My wife and kids and I stood around the great pine, holding hands, and I said a simple prayer: "Dear God, we ask that everyone who sees this tree will see God in it." My wife asked me afterward who in the world I thought would see this old tree in the center of a cow pasture, in the middle of nowhere. I told her I wasn't sure why I had said that prayer; it just came out. With the consecration of that tree, however, things seemed to be put into motion.

I began traveling to Medjugorje frequently and my sporadic writings turned into regular communications for a growing readership. Everything I wrote was signed by the name "A Friend of Medjugorje," because I did not wish to bring glory to my name, especially in light of Our Lady's words to me to "live in humility." I was taking people on pilgrimages to Medjugorje and I got to know the visionaries, developing a close friendship in particular with Marija. In 1988, on one of these pilgrimages, I passed by the office of Father Slavko where the visions had been taking place. I noticed Father was packing up his office because he was being transferred. I volunteered to help him pack, which took most of the afternoon. When we were finished, Father took the crucifix off the wall—the one the visionaries would kneel before during hundreds of apparitions—and told me that he wanted me to have it. I was astonished and refused to accept such a sacred object, saying that it belonged to someone worthier. But Father would not take no for an answer. He was so insistent that I took the crucifix and immediately brought it to Marija. I asked her to pray over it that it would serve as a tool of conversion for our nation. Maria took the crucifix lovingly, praying over it with her whole heart, and kissed it gently.

I brought this magnificent treasure home to Alabama and showed it to Annette. I told her we needed to pray to discern where in our home to hang such a special gift in order to give it the honor it deserved. We walked around the house, praying the Rosary, but no inspiration came. As a convert to the faith, my wife had only one condition: that the crucifix was not hung over our bed. When we could not determine where to hang it, we decided to put it away on a shelf next to our fireplace until we gained further clarification.

In October that year, I returned to Medjugorje to discover Marija quite upset. I tried to find out what was wrong. Marija started telling me that her brother had been diagnosed with kidney disease and that there was no help for him in Medjugorje or anywhere in their country for that matter. She was willing and able to donate one of her own kidneys, but there was no place to perform such an operation. As she poured out her heart to me, I was stunned, not about what Marija was saying, but how she was saying it. A month earlier, she could not speak English. And here she was speaking perfect English, using words like "kidney dialysis" and other medical terminology. I finally stopped her and asked when she had learned to speak English so well. Marija looked at me with complete surprise and said she didn't know she was even speaking English. At that moment I knew I had been meant to hear this conversation, but I didn't know what I was supposed to do with it. On my trip home, landing at the airport, I saw a newspaper in the newsstand. On the front page was an article about Birmingham having the leading hospital in the world for kidney transplants.

I suddenly became very excited, wondering if this was Our Lady's way of telling me that she desired to appear in Alabama. I began to pray fervently. I contacted the hospital and had to go through a lot of red tape, but I finally was able to call Marija and tell her that the operation could be done in Birmingham if she and her brother wanted to come. She agreed, and I made the arrangements. The other half of the miracle was that Marija and her brother were able to obtain visas. This was a difficult process in a Communist country, and in those days it was unheard of for the visionaries to leave their homeland.

Some time before this, the man who owned the field adjacent to our home passed away. The land fell into the hands of his son-in-law, who had always been jealous of my relationship with his father-in-law. We had desired to buy the field for five years, but by now it had become a power-ful urge because I had discerned that the field was important for reasons not yet revealed to me. I prayed hard, and God encouraged me to approach the young man about selling the land, but he refused. I tried several times, but the man was hostile. Finally, I gave up and left for Medjugorje to see if Marija still wanted to follow through with the operation in this country.

While I was in Medjugorje, Annette had a vivid dream that she was supposed to hang the crucifix from Father Slavko over our bed. The dream was so vivid, it woke her up. She couldn't imagine where this idea was coming from and tried to go back to sleep. Again she was awakened with the same thought. When this happened a third time, Annette realized that this was meant to be, and at the same time she had an impulse to bring a little statue of Our Lady of Fatima into the bedroom as well. She was burning with excitement about the whole idea and could not go back to sleep. At the first rays of light she woke the children and together they hung the crucifix as directed.

Annette and I had discussed beforehand where the apparitions should take place if Marija should come to Alabama and we both thought it appropriate that they happen at the local parish. The evening I arrived with Marija and her brother it was very late and we all went to bed. At six o'clock the next morning, I was awakened by a knock on the door. It was the wife of the son-in-law who owned the field. Apparently, they had some serious financial needs and would sell the field immediately. I signed the contract then and there.

That morning we hurried to get dressed. We drove to the local parish, but once we got there Marija seemed to get the impression that the apparitions would not take place here. We were running out of time, so we raced back home. I let Marija walk through the house to decide where she would welcome Our Lady. As soon as she walked into our bedroom and saw the crucifix, she announced with conviction that this was the place the apparitions would happen. Annette and I looked at each other in dismay—this would have been the last place we would have selected. Who invites anyone to the bedroom? But we submitted to Our Lady's will and for the next two and a half months she appeared to Maria there, giving daily messages including three monthly messages for the world.

Word got out pretty fast that there was a visionary from Medjugorje having her apparitions in our home. It was exciting to see how many people came to the house, but it was overwhelming at the same time. People came in and stayed all day, visiting our bedroom and longing to speak to Marija and be in the presence of Our Lady. Hundreds gathered in the adjacent field. There was some negative reaction as well, and the bishop's office received many calls. After looking into the matter, he decided that as long as the crowds were gathering to pray on the field, it was permissible.

Since I had acquired the field at the beginning of Marija's visit, I asked Marija to invite the Blessed Mother to appear there for the benefit of those gathered under the tree in prayer during the time of the apparitions. Our Lady was silent about this matter until one day she told Marija that she would appear in the field the next day and that everyone was invited to come. The next day was November 24, 1988, Thanksgiving Day. We had actually forgotten all about Thanksgiving due to the hectic schedule and enormous crowds. In retrospect, I feel strongly that this date was no accident. Thanksgiving is a significant day for our nation: it is the day we celebrate our roots, our feast day to celebrate our Christian foundation, and a time to thank God for our blessings. On that cold November day, Our Lady appeared under the lone pine tree that we consecrated years before, in the presence of a multitude, in the middle of nowhere.

It was during the apparitions in late 1988 that Marija told me she believed Our Lady desired a community to be established here in Alabama. I had no idea how to do this, and I wasn't sure I wanted to be the one to have to choose who was in and who was not. In time, I understood that God was calling us through Our Lady to live in a certain way, and that anyone who wished to live in this manner could become a part of the community. And so a community was birthed, one that at first consisted of just my family. As it evolved and became known, it took the name of our mission, Caritas of Birmingham, because *caritas* is the Latin word for love and charity.

After Marija's visit to this country and the blessings of the apparitions, Satan was allowed to be unleashed on me and I went through a great deal of suffering. There were people who wanted to close down the field because they didn't believe in any of it. Others were angry because they thought it was taking away from Medjugorje. A caustic jealousy arose, resulting in many persecutions. I desperately needed Our Lady to speak to me through Marija, but the only answer I received was *"Pray."* I was in Medjugorje with my family for a month and I prayed fervently. Again I asked Marija to approach Our Lady, and again the answer came: *"Pray."* I was frustrated, because I needed more clarity. Marija suggested that we say a nine-day novena together at five o'clock in the morning atop Mt. Krizevac, because Our Lady loved this type of prayer. This time the answer came back: *"You pray. You are in a time of prayer."*

I was more satisfied with this response and I returned home and changed the focus of my newsletter. Instead of stories about Medjugorje, my writings focused on the messages and what was being revealed to me through much prayer, in particular how the messages pertained to family life. People began to come to Birmingham and join our little community. Singles came, and then a few families. We grew slowly, but with a solid foundation of prayer, fasting, scripture, and the sacraments. Our purpose was simply to dedicate ourselves to living and spreading the messages of Medjugorje.

In 1995, I visited Marija and her family in Italy. On the Feast of the Visitation, I knelt beside Marija during her apparition. As she got up to write something down, Marija told me to start praying the Magnificat. I had not asked Marija to ask any questions of the Blessed Mother. Regardless, there was a message for me and the community: *"Little children, I desire that through your lives you are witnesses, that you are my extended hands, my instruments. Get as many hearts as you can close to my heart and lead them to God, to a way of salvation."*

The following year I traveled to Rome in an attempt to see Pope John Paul II about our mission. The community at home prayed hard for this intention. When I could not get in to see him, I ended up talking to a Swiss Guard and telling him how I wanted to meet the Holy Father. To my surprise, he glanced quickly down both directions of the corridor and scribbled something on a piece of paper. He handed it to me: it was the fax number to the pope's private office. I faxed a letter saying that I was simply a husband and a father, but I would consider it a great honor to meet with the Holy Father. I received a call from the pope's secretary to come the next day at four o'clock in the morning. I was escorted through chamber after chamber to the chapel where Mass was going to be held for the pontiff. Someone approached me and asked if I would like to do the reading for the day. I was stupefied to be given such an honor. Entering the chapel, I saw an ornate chair in the middle of the room facing the altar that I assumed must be for the pope. After praying for a while two feet from this chair, I realized that the Holy Father was already sitting in it. The words I proclaimed from scripture that morning overwhelmed me: "I brought you through chamber after chamber to set you before my High Priest." I don't remember anything else from the reading. Afterward, I met with Pope John Paul II and told him about our mission back home in Alabama. I received three blessings from him that day. He gave one to me, one to my family, and one to the community.

Despite the persecutions, rumors, and oppression we have faced for the past fifteen years, our community continues to grow in peace and love and simplicity. Under Our Lady's ever-present guidance, we have opened a Mission House in Medjugorje—a second community—and from our two locations we welcome visitors and distribute newsletters, books, audiotapes, and other materials to all who seek it. We host pilgrimages to Medjugorje and days of retreat at Caritas, where thousands of people join us in prayer in the field to consecrate our nation back to God. Marija has returned to Alabama a number of times since her first visit, each time gracing us with the presence of the Blessed Mother.

Our Lady has shown our community a joyful, prayerful way of life that allows us to live first for God and, by doing so, to lead others to Him. It is family life the way God intended it, working side by side in a common effort. We study and live the messages as a witness to the world to help it in its conversion, much like the early Christians did. Recently, we have birthed a plan for an Extended Community in which we are inviting people from all walks of life to share in our mission by participating in various levels of prayer, fasting, and scripture study without actually living in community with us. We believe this is how Our Lady intends to spread "her way" to the ends of the earth, transforming it under the protection of her motherly mantle. Living this "way" has led to a deeper living of the Gospel and our every effort is in harmony with the call for evangelization from our Mother Church, to whom we are in complete submission. Through the grace of Our Lord and Our

Lady, millions of people around the world have been exposed to Medjugorje through the work of this simple community—a community of family, faith, and love.

Terry Colafrancesco, c.o.c.i., Alabama

"Dear children, today I wish to place you all under my mantle to protect you from every satanic attack. Today is the day of peace, but throughout the whole world there is much lack of peace. Therefore, I call you to build up a new world of peace together with me, by means of prayer. Without you, I cannot do that, and, therefore, I call all of you, with my motherly love, and God will do the rest. Therefore, open yourselves to God's plans and purposes for you to be able to cooperate with Him for peace and for good. And do not forget that your life does not belong to you, but is a gift with which you must bring joy to others and lead them to Eternal Life. May the tenderness of little Jesus always accompany you. Thank you for having responded to my call."

Message of December 25, 1992

Suggested Reading

The following titles are recommended to enhance your knowledge of the apparitions of Medjugorje. It is by no means a comprehensive or definitive listing.

Barbaric, Slavko. *Pray with the Heart: The Medjugorje Manual of Prayer.* Distributed by Franciscan University Press, Steubenville, OH, 1988.

Beyer, Richard. *Medjugorje Day by Day: A Daily Meditation Book Based on the Messages of Our Lady of Medjugorje.* Notre Dame, IN: Ave Maria Press, 1993.

Connell, Janice. *Queen of the Cosmos: Interviews with the Visionaries of Medjugorje.* Orleans, MA: Paraclete Press, 1990.

Connell, Janice. *Visions of the Children: The Apparitions of the Blessed Mother at Medjugorje.* New York: St. Martin's Press, 1992.

Friend of Medjugorje. *Words from Heaven: Messages of Our Lady from Medjugorje.* Birmingham, AL: St. James Publishing, 2003.

Kraljevic, Svetozar. *Pilgrimage.* Orleans, MA: Paraclete Press, 1993.

Maillard, Emmanuel. *Medjugorje: The 90s.* Santa Barbara, CA: Queenship Publishing Company, 1999.

Weible, Wayne. *Final Harvest: Medjugorje at the End of the Century.* Orleans, MA: Paraclete Press, 1999.

———. *Letters from Medjugorje.* Orleans, MA: Paraclete Press, 1991.

———. *Medjugorje the Message.* Orleans, MA: Paraclete Press, 1989.

———. *Medjugorje the Mission.* Orleans, MA: Paraclete Press, 1995.

Contact Information

Many of the testimonials in this book discuss products, services, and organizations related to and inspired by living the messages of the apparitions of Medjugorje. The following is a list of detailed contact information for your convenience.

"True Freedom" (page 15)
To order a video copy of Jim Jennings' conversion story, or for other information about Medjugorje, please contact The MIR Group, One Galleria Boulevard, Suite 744, Metairie, LA 70001; Mimi Kelly, Director; Phone: (504) 849-2570, FAX: (504) 849-2574, Message line: (504) 849-2572; E-mail: themirgroup@aol.com; Web site: http://www.themirgroup.org.

"Carry My Messages" (page 29)
To subscribe to *The Spirit of Medjugorje Newsletter,* please contact Editor June Klins at tnklins@velocity.net; (814) 898-2143; or P.O. Box 6614, Erie, PA 16512.

"Illuminate All Souls" (page 34)
To order videos by Sean Bloomfield, or for other information about Medjugorje, please visit www.medjugorjevideo.com.

"Renewing the Church" (page 64)
To subscribe to *Medjugorje Magazine*, please call (630) 968-4684, or write to P.O. Box 373, Westmont, IL 60559-0373. You can also visit their Web site at: www.medjugormag.com. For conference schedules or other materials, contact the DuPage Marian Center at 317 West Ogden Avenue, Westmont, IL 60559. Phone: (630) 968-5268.

"The Way" (page 75)
For more information on Monica Ursino, singer and songwriter, to order her music or for a schedule of where she is playing, visit her Web site at: www.MonicaUrsino.com.

"Works of Mercy" (page 82)
St. Luke's Mission of Mercy welcomes the support of time, talent, finance, and prayer. For more information, contact St. Luke's Mission of Mercy at: 325 Walden Avenue, Buffalo, NY 14211 or call (716) 894-4476.

"Meeting People Where They Are" (page 115)
For more information about the music of Jamie Marich and Cornersburg Music (ASCAP), contact www.jamiemarich.com; info@jamiemarich.com; or cornersburg@yahoo.com; or call (330) 881-2944. Jamie's CDs are available at: www.cdbaby.com/marich.

"River of Love" (page 125)
Visit the Medjugorje Web at www.medjugorje.org or contact us at: The Medjugorje Web, 772 Peace Road, DeKalb, IL 60115. Phone: (815) 748-0410.

"In Your Arms" (page 147)
To support St. David's Relief Foundation, or for more information, visit their Web site at: www.stdavids.org. You may

also contact them at: St. David's Relief Foundation at 4355 Highway 67 East, Suite 101, Mesquite, TX 75150, or by calling (800) 618-9789.

"Two Hearts" (page 169)

For more information about The Order of the Sacred and Immaculate Hearts of Jesus and Mary, please write to them at: 48765 Annapolis Road, Hopedale, OH 43976 or call (740) 946-9000.

"Coins for the Master" (page 175)

For complete information on the apparitions of Medjugorje, including messages, pilgrimages, conversion stories, news, and events, or to order Michael's new book, *Medjugorje Investigated,* visit www.MedjugorjeUSA.com.

"Instruments of Peace" (page 197)

For more information on helping the Queen of Peace Catholic Schools, contact Anna Karczemska at: annak@mail.p.lodz.pl in Poland, or write her at: ul. Armii Krajowej 44/43, 94-046 Lodz POLAND or call 011 48 603 675 733. Or, contact Reverend Eugeniusz Spiolek at Fire of God's Peace (Ognisko Bozego Pokoju), at: ul. Gdanska 85, 80-613 Lodz POLAND or call +48 42 636 30 77. In the U.S., contact Carolanne Kilichowski at 8159 Boston State Road, Hamburg, NY 14075, call (716) 941-9256, or e-mail magdziak@peoplepc. com.

"People of Peace and Love" (page 202)

For more information about the Sisters of the Sick Poor of Los Angeles, e-mail us at VocationsDirector@Sistersofthe SickPoor.org, call them at (310) 415-2563, or write them at: Sisters of the Sick Poor of Los Angeles, Sister Laura Maripaz

Sanchez, Vocational Director, 3570 Brenton Avenue, Apt. E, Lynwood, CA 90262. You can also visit their Web site at: www.sistersofthesickpoor.org.

"Food Where There Is Hunger" (page 213)
Medjugorje International Relief welcomes prayers, publicity, volunteerism, and donations. For more information, please visit their Web site at: www.manchestermedjugorje.cjb.net or contact them at: Medjugorje International Relief, c/o 13, Erlington Avenue, Old Trafford, Manchester M16 0FN. UK. Phone: (UK) 0161 881 5664; e-mail: mirmedjugorje@aol.com.

"Community of Love" (page 220)
To learn more about the Community of Caritas or the Extended Caritas Community, or to receive their newsletter or a catalog of books, tapes, and other materials, please contact Caritas of Birmingham, 100 Our Lady Queen of Peace Drive, Sterrett, AL 35147-9987, or call (205) 672-2000.

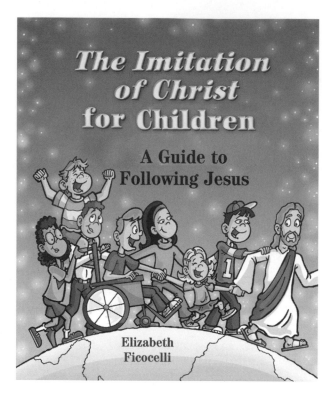